Contemporary Arab World

Literary and Linguistic Issues

EDITED BY

BARBARA MICHALAK-PIKULSKA

Jagiellonian University Press

Reviewer
Prof. dr hab. Adnan Abbas

Cover design
Marta Jaszczuk

The publication is financed by the Jagiellonian University from the funds of the Institute of Oriental Studies of the Faculty of Philology

ISBN 978-83-233-4933-4
ISBN 978-83-233-7179-3 (e-book)

JAGIELLONIAN
UNIVERSITY
PRESS

www.wuj.pl

Jagiellonian University Press
Editorial Offices: Michałowskiego 9/2, 31-126 Kraków
Phone: +48 12 663 23 80, Fax: +48 12 663 23 83
Distribution: Phone: +48 12 631 01 97, Fax: +48 12 631 01 98
Cell Phone: + 48 506 006 674, e-mail: sprzedaz@wuj.pl
Bank: PEKAO SA, IBAN PL 80 1240 4722 1111 0000 4856 3325

Contents

اللغة

Introduction

Publication entitled *The Contemporary Arab World. Literary and Linguistic Issues* was designed and written by the members of staff of the Department of Arabic Studies of the Jagiellonian University in Kraków. It shows results of the research linked to their scholarly and didactic interests. It is a collection of six papers dealing with selected issues in the field of Arabic language and literature, focused on phenomena and processes taking place in contemporary Arab world.

Teaching Arabic as a foreign language faces many methodological challenges connected with the specificity and complexity of the sociolinguistic situation in the Arab world. They mostly concern the necessity for considering different types (registers) of the language, distinguishing, understanding and using which makes it possible for learners to achieve full communication skills.

The end of the 20th and the beginning of the 21st century brought above all a new look at the didactic process, forcing revision of the traditional grammar – translation method in teaching foreign languages. Higher education schools must cope with new problems connected with their functioning on the broad market of formal and informal education, which is determined by the term "success on the job market". Needs and expectations of learners change. Which direction will development of Arabic Studies take then? How to bring together the mission of higher education institutions and pragmatic needs of the market, or current needs of "consumers" and guidelines of central curricula. Is such compromise possible?

The main area of reflection in the chapter *Between past achievements and future challenges* by Agnieszka Pałka-Lasek is going to be the issues connected with university didactics on the example of the Jagiellonian University in Krakow and its Department of Arabic Studies.

In the chapter *Meanings and functions of genitive constructions in Modern Standard Arabic* Iwona Król discusses genitive constructions containing substantives as well as adjectives and numerals as nomen regens and substantives as nomen rectum. In all these groups of genitival phrases their determined components precede determiners, and irrespective of part of speech they represent, they follow syntactic rules of a substantive. The grammatical properties of nomen rectum are determined by the meaning of the whole phrase or by syntactic demands within the sentence. The paper is aimed at determining general meanings of particular constructions of the same formal type. Numerous examples gathered here may be useful for university teaching.

In the chapter entitled *Sultan Qaboos – image of the ruler in panegyrics and elegies by Omani poets* Barbara Michalak-Pikulska presents selected panegyrics by Sa'īda bint Khāṭir al-Fārisī, Turkiyya al-Būsa'īdī, and Ṣāliḥ al-Fahdī written in honor of Sultan Qaboos during his five decades of rule and elegies by Sa'īd aṣ-Ṣaqlāwī, Hilāl bin Sayf ash-Shiyādī, and Aḥmad bin Hilāl al-'Abrī which appeared in the Omani press after his death on January 10, 2020. They show how much one of the longest reigning rulers in the world enjoyed love and authority. The Omani loved him because he always put their welfare first and Oman flourished. His reign is considered a golden period in the history of the country.

Microfiction, flash fiction or very short story in modern Arabic literature by Yousef Sh'hadeh focuses on examining and analysing various examples from the works of three writers whose stories have expressed the extent of development of this new art, and its constancy as a literary genre clearly defined in modern Arabic prose. The stories studied are samples of works by writers from different Arab countries: Maḥmūd Shuqayr (Palestine), Ibrāhīm Darġūthī (Tunisia), and Muḥammad Ḥijjū (Morocco).

In the chapter *In the maze of discourses – monodrama Bāy bāy Ğīllū (Bye Bye Gillo) by Ṭaha 'Adnān* Sebastian Gadomski through the analysis of a theatrical play written by the Moroccan author tries to show pluralism and a multitude of discourses that shape our place in the world and influence our life stories. A wide spectrum of issues related to the question of discourse and its critical analysis is the background for the discussion contained in the chapter.

The chapter *Women in Islamic State propaganda* by Marcin Gajec focuses on presenting the efforts of propaganda specialists directed at women. The online magazines Dabiq and Rumiyah or the Al-Khansa Brigade's online manifesto are excellent examples of such activities and allow to trace significant differences in the message addressed to European women and to the inhabitants of the Middle East.

We hope that these articles will contribute to the enrichment of knowledge about the Arab world.

Authors

AGNIESZKA PAŁKA-LASEK

Between past achievements and future challenges

Arabic language teaching at the university level – example of the Department of Arabic Studies at the Jagiellonian University in Cracow

Introduction

Teaching Arabic as a foreign language is connected with numerous methodology related challenges, and most of them result from the specificity and complexity of the socio-linguistic situation in the Arab world. However, methodology related problems, which remain an open issue and leave the door wide open for discussion, are not the only dilemmas that university level language teaching is facing nowadays. The needs and expectations of learners are changing. The view on the broadly understood sense of higher education and the value of education itself are changing. The teaching market is changing. What are the problems that teaching Arabic at 21st century universities has to face? What are the challenges we are facing and what new windows can be open for higher education?

The issue of legal frameworks, which also play an important role in the teaching process at academic level, is raised very rarely in these debates. Despite some degree of autonomy, which results from the extensive statutory rights of the universities as entities, language education at universities is part of formal education and as such it is subject to strict normative rules, resulting from national and international legal acts, which in turn are a derivative of general education policy. This aspect of teaching is highlighted in the article written by Jerzy Łacina,[1] defining it as so-called "supervisor's expectations", which can significantly affect the didactic process. This issue will also appear many times in the considerations presented here about the realities of teaching Arabic language in Poland.

The beginnings of European Arabist research go back to the 11th century and are closely related to translation activities.[2] Probably also in the middle of the 12th century the translation schools were operating in Toledo.[3] The first chairs of Arabic began to arise in the 16th century – in 1538 François I founded a chair in Arabic at the Collège royal in Paris, in 1599 a chair in Arabic at Leiden University was established.[4] However in Poland, for many decades the interest in Arab culture was informal and was inspired – as can be easily guessed – somehow by pragmatic reasons. Among the enthusiasts of the Eastern world there were, among others: travelers, politicians or experts in various fields which were unrelated to philology, such as doctors,[5] whose written testimonials have undoubtedly enriched the Polish intellectual heritage, although they were not of a scientific nature except for a few examples. Knowledge of Arabic language was rare, the sources document few more or less correct sample quotes and indicate the functioning of borrowings. Similarly, the Romantic era fascination with the Orient was primarily reflected in processing of Eastern motifs in literature and fine arts, however, it was the 19th century that opened the history of Polish Oriental studies.[6] This is also when the history of teaching Arabic at Polish universities began. The first Department of Eastern Languages and Oriental Literature in Poland was created at the Jagiellonian University. In 2019, the Jagiellonian University Institute of Oriental Studies celebrated its centenary. The Institute initiated its work in 1919, and Arabic language studies were one of the basic research areas from the very beginning. During the

---

1 J. Łacina, *Kulturowo-techniczne problemy dydaktyki języka arabskiego na początku XXI wieku – nowe wyzwania*, in: B. Michalak-Pikulska, M. Lewicka (eds.), *Dydaktyka języka arabskiego*, Wydawnictwo Naukowe Uniwersytetu Mikołaja Kopernika, Toruń 2013, p. 31 et seq.

2 J. Danecki, *Gramatyka języka arabskiego*, Wydawnictwo Akademickie Dialog, Warszawa 1994, p. 46.

3 A. Hamilton, *Arabic Studies in Europe*, in: K. Versteeg, *Encyclopedia of Arabic Language and Linguistics*, E.J. Brill, Leiden 2011, p. 171.

4 Ibid.

5 See among others J. Potocki, *Voyage en Turquie et en Egypte fait en 1784*, Warszawa 1788; idem, *Voyage dans l'Empire de Maroc, fait en l'année 1791. Suivi du Voyage de Hafez, récit oriental*, Warszawa 1792; S. Pilsztynowa, *Proceder podróży i życia mego awantur*, Wydawnictwo Literackie, Kraków 1957.

6 See Wojciech Kazimirski-Biberstein.

period of its activity, the Department has gained an indisputable reputation on the international scientific arena, and has also significantly developed its teaching mission. The 100th anniversary jubilee may become an inspiration for a brief reflection on the condition of Oriental education at the academic level, especially on the didactics of the Arabic language. A brief look at the history and present day of the Cracow Department of Arabic Studies will serve as a starting point for broader considerations on the practice of teaching Arabic language at universities.

1. History of Arabic language teaching at the Jagiellonian University

In the jubilee memories of the history of Oriental studies at the Jagiellonian University in the monograph *Języki i cywilizacje*,[7] K. Paraskiewicz[8] indicates significant events that set the basic stages in the formation of Cracow's Arabic studies, starting from the creation of the aforementioned Department of Eastern Languages and Oriental Literature. The Department has been operated since 1818, and its mentor, the German scholar Wilhelm Münnich, was the first professor of Eastern literature at the Jagiellonian University. He managed the chair until 1826. The study programme covered learning of several Semitic languages, including Arabic language and Oriental literature. Classes were addressed to students of the Faculty of Philosophy, Faculty of Law and Theology (in practice, their number did not exceed ten people). After the transfer of Professor Münnich to the University of Vilnius, the cathedral was dissolved.

The semitological research was resumed only in 1911. In 1914, the habilitation of Tadeusz Kowalski[9] took place at the Jagiellonian University based on the development of a collection of poems of Qais ibn al-Ḫaṭīm *Der Dīwān des Ḳais ibn al-Ḫaṭīm*. Tadeusz Kowalski's habilitation was the first habilitation in the field of Arabic studies in the history of Polish

7 J. Świt (ed.), *Języki i cywilizacje*, Wydział Filologiczny Uniwersytetu Jagiellońskiego – Wydawnictwo Nowa Strona, Kraków–Bielsko Biała 2019.

8 K. Paraskiewicz, *Z historii orientalistyki w Uniwersytecie Jagiellońskim*, in: J. Świt (ed.), *Języki i cywilizacje*, pp. 15–34.

9 For more on the activities of Cracow Orientalists, see K. Paraskiewicz, *Orientaliści krakowscy*, in: L. Sudyka (ed.), *Orientalia Commemorativa*, Wydawnictwo Uniwersytetu Jagiellońskiego, Kraków 2011, pp. 75–88.

science, and it was Professor Tadeusz Kowalski who is widely recognized as the creator of Polish Oriental studies. In 1915 Assistant Professor Kowalski began teaching Arabic in the form of lectures (in addition to Arabic, Kowalski – who was Arabist, Iranian and Turkologist, also lectured on Persian and Ottoman Turkish as well as the history of the Muslim East). On July 1919, already holding the title of associate professor, he took over the first Department of Oriental Philology in independent Poland, which was established by the decree of the head of state, Józef Piłsudski. The didactic activity of the department was interrupted by World War II. It was resumed in March 1945. The first post-war academic year lasted only a trimester. It was not until the 1945/46 academic year that the full-time teaching process was ensured. As a comprehensively educated orientalist-philologist, but also a committed pedagogue, Professor Kowalski postulated the need to teach Eastern languages also in other universities. From 1928 until the outbreak of war, he taught Arabic, Turkish and Persian at the University of Commerce, from which the current University of Economics was developed. The oriental students of the Jagiellonian University had to attend these classes.

In the abovementioned monograph, J. Pisowicz[10] notes that the oriental studies in terms of methodology drew mainly from the research apparatus on the so-called "dead languages" and mainly focused on developing the passive understanding of the source texts.[11] It should be emphasized that at this stage, researchers often looked at teaching Eastern languages from the comparative linguistics' point of view. Thus, Arabic was only one of the languages taught in the broad field of the Oriental studies.

A definite change in the formula of Oriental studies was brought by the term of the medievalist historian and Arabist – professor Tadeusz Lewicki, who took over the chair after the death of professor Kowalski in 1948. As K. Paraskiewicz writes, a reform of university studies and then the renaming of the Department of Oriental Philology in 1972 to the Institute of Oriental Studies allowed Professor Lewicki to have structural transformations undergone and to create a broader scientific unit with specialised subunits.[12] It was when three specialties: Arabic, Turkological and Iranian ones emerged within the Institute, and on 1 June 1972, the Arabic,

---

10 A. Pisowicz, *Stulecie krakowskiej orientalistyki*, in: J. Świt (ed.), *Języki i cywilizacje*, pp. 7–13.

11 Ibid., p. 11.

12 K. Paraskiewicz, *Z historii orientalistyki w Uniwersytecie Jagiellońskim*, p. 20.

Iranian and Turkology departments were created (the unit also continued research in the field of African studies and the studies in the field of numismatics and research on oriental sources). Additional scientific and teaching staff was employed. The study program was also expanded. The number of classes was over 30; unfortunately the number of language classes did not increase. As in the previous period, the Oriental studies also educated no more than six-eight students a year. One of the important problems was the inability to travel abroad, which was related to the political situation in Poland, however, since the 1950s, the unit has also employed Arabic native speakers as language teachers.[13] Since then, the linguistic pragmatics, including contact with live language, have become one of the key determinants of Cracow's Arabic studies. After the retirement of Professor Lewicki in 1976, Andrzej Czapkiewicz took over the management of the Department of Arabic Studies. In this period there were two main areas of research interest: dialectology and history of Arabic linguistics. With the further history of Cracow Arabic studies there are associated the following scholars: Professors Maria Kowalska, Andrzej Zaborski and Elżbieta Górska. In the 1990s, the number of hours of literary language learning was significantly increased and teaching of dialects was introduced. In 2004, the Department of Arabic Studies was transformed into a Chair of Arabic Studies.[14] Since 1999 Professor Barbara Michalak-Pikulska, a specialist in the modern Arabic Literature, acts as the Head of the unit.

2. Problems of modern Arabic didactics

2.1. Subject and teaching methods

Discussions on the subject of Arabic language didactics in the academic circles focus mainly on two issues – the subject of teaching (problem of diglossia[15] – Arabic literary language versus dialects) and widely understood

---

[13] A. Pisowicz, *Stulecie krakowskiej orientalistyki*, p. 12.

[14] For more on Arabic studies in Cracow, see B. Michalak-Pikulska, *Studia arabistyczne w Krakowie*, in: L. Sudyka (ed.), *Orientalia Commemorativa*, pp. 43–48.

[15] Diglossia – "a relatively stable language situation in which, in addition to the primary dialects (which may include a standard or regional standards), there is a very divergent, highly codified (often grammatically more complex) superposed variety, the vehicle of a large and respected body of written literature, either of an either period

methodology. The first and basic question teachers of the Arabic language ask themselves is: *What do we really teach or should teach?*

Ongoing works on the broadly understood in this way method for teaching Arabic have been in progress since the 1960's,[16] just to mention some authors like Mitchell,[17] Abboud[18] or Tapiero.[19] Apart from two traditional teaching methods: the Modern Standard Arabic teaching method based on teaching grammar rules and reading texts, and the everyday language teaching method based on teaching utterances (i.e. one of the dialects of a group of dialects[20]), most contemporary didactic compilations account for simultaneous teaching of both. In Poland, the Arabic language curriculum for students of Arabic Studies at Polish universities was developed at the Jagiellonian University and published as *Didactics of Arabic Language* by E. Górska and M. Skoczek in 1999.[21] The curriculum, with some

---

or in another speech community, which is learned largely by formal education and is used for most written and formal spoken purposes but is not used by any sector of the community for ordinary conversation". Ch.A. Ferguson, *Diglossia*, "Word" 1959, 15, p. 336. See also W. Marçais, *La diglossie arabe*, "L'enseigment public" 1930, 97, pp. 401–409; A.S. Nalborczyk, *Zachowania językowe imigrantów arabskich w Austrii*, Wydawnictwo Akademickie Dialog, Warszawa 2003.

16 The first Polish publication related to this issue was the article of A. Parzymies, *L'enseignement de l'arabe littéral face à la diglossie*, in: R.T. Nasr (ed.), *The Teaching of Arabic to Adults in Europe (Proceedings of the 14th AIMAV Seminar, 23–25 May 1983, Collection d'Études Linguistiques*, 32), AIMAV, Bruxelles 1983, pp. 29–35. See also E. Górska, *Wybrane zagadnienia dydaktyki uniwersyteckiej języka arabskiego*, "Biuletyn Glottodydaktyczny" (Kraków) 2003, 9–10, pp. 135–140; M. Al-Sayadi, *Język literacki oraz dialekty w dydaktyce języka arabskiego. Kayfa ḥāluka czy keyf ḥālek?*, in: B. Michalak-Pikulska, M. Lewicka (eds.), *Dydaktyka języka arabskiego*, pp. 197–207.

17 T.F. Mitchell, *The Teaching of Arabic in Great Britain, Linguistic Report*, "Newsletter of the Center for Applied Linguistics" (Washington) 1969, 11/2 (April), Suppl. 20.

18 P.F. Abboud, *The Teaching of Arabic in the United States. The State of the Art*, Center for Applied Linguistics, Washington, DC 1968.

19 N. Tapiero, *Pour une didatique de l'arabe moderne, langue de communication: problématique et solution*, v. I–II, Lille–Paris 1976.

20 For more on Arabic variants, see among others: M. Badawi El-Said, *Educated Spoken Arabic: A Problem in Teaching Arabic as a Foreign Language*, in: K. Jankowsky (ed.), *Scientific and Humanistic Dimensions of Language*, John Benjamins, Amsterdam–Philadelphia 1985; Ch. Blanc, *Style Variations in Spoken Arabic: A Sample of Interdialectical Educated Conversation*, in: A.Ch. Ferguson at al. (eds.), *Contribution to Arabic Linguistics*, Harvard University Press, Cambridge 1960, pp. 81–158; J. Blau, *Studies in Middle Arabic and Its Judaeo-Arabic Variety*, Magnes Press, Jerusalem 1988; J. Danecki, *Współczesny język arabski i jego dialekty*, Wydawnictwo Akademickie Dialog, Warszawa 2000.

21 E. Górska, M. Skoczek, A. Hasan, *Dydaktyka języka arabskiego*, Wydawnictwo Akademickie Dialog, Warszawa 1999.

modifications, still constitutes the basis for teaching the language at Cracow Arabic Studies.

One of undoubtedly most important events in higher education over the last years was the introduction of the Act of 18th March 2011 on the amendment to the act Higher Education Law.[22] This brought about the need to verify current curricula,[23] but most of all changed the way education process is perceived and described on higher education level. The main reasons for the Reform were: increase in mobility of EU citizens, including students and graduates of universities and other types of schools, related to the increasing offer of exchange programs and opening of labour markets, increasing awareness of the need for lifelong learning, increasing universality of higher education. The fundamental assumption of the Reform was changing the perception of the educational process from an education system based on teaching the curriculum content to a system based on the implementation of specific learning outcomes, including a set of general skills (useful regardless of your career path) and those related to the major of studies. The effects were described in three categories: knowledge, skills and social competence. This otherwise pragmatic approach to the goals of teaching at the level of higher education did not interfere with the distinction of two so-called education profiles – a practical profile for students to acquire practical skills and a general academic profile covering the module of classes used to acquire "in-depth theoretical skills" by a student (Art. 2 clause 1 item 18e of the Act), provided that it is the latter one that should be considered fundamental for the curricula of research units. This implies a philological approach to language learning.

The point of reference was the publication of the *Common European Framework of Reference for Languages: Learning, Teaching, Assessment*[24] by the Language Policy Division of the European Council in 2001. It shifted the educational balance point from strictly linguistic knowledge

---

[22] See provisions of the act Ustawa z dnia 18 marca 2011 r. o zmianie ustawy – Prawo o szkolnictwie wyższym, ustawy o stopniach naukowych i tytule naukowym oraz o stopniach i tytule w zakresie sztuki oraz o zmianie niektórych innych ustaw (Dz.U. z 2011 r. Nr 84, poz. 455).

[23] The implementation of the Reform guidelines involved the adaptation to the requirements of amendments to internal university regulations (such as the mode for creating and removing the individual types of studies), verification of the offer of study courses conducted by individual university units, and finally the modification of the curricula themselves.

[24] Council of Europe, *Common European Framework of Reference for Languages: Learning, Teaching, Assessment*, 2011.

(systemic knowledge of language) to the development of broadly defined "competences" (including, apart from language competences, general competences, those not specific to language, but which are called upon for actions of all kinds, including language activities). According to the definition, competences are "the sum of descriptive knowledge, skills and characteristics that allow a person to perform actions". The basic term "language competence" was replaced with a more broad term "communicative language competences" which consists of three components: sociolinguistic one, linguistic one and a pragmatic one. Only when combined do these competences enable undertaking various language activities. Therefore, language teaching process accounts for taking actions on three levels: acquisition of knowledge, skills and some specific social competencies. One of the most important elements of the Reform, initiated this way, was the introduction of the so-called National Qualification Framework, the method of describing qualifications acquired in the national higher education system based on European standards.

The problem, however, is the very necessity for reference to the European Language Education Description System, widely used in language certification.

For example, at the language level B (Independet user), required to achieve undergraduate studies, the learner:

B1 (Threshold or intermediate)

- Can understand the main points of clear standard input on familiar matters regularly encountered in work, school, leisure, etc.
- Can deal with most situations likely to arise while travelling in an area where the language is spoken.
- Can produce simple connected text on topics that are familiar or of personal interest.
- Can describe experiences and events, dreams, hopes and ambitions and briefly give reasons and explanations for opinions and plans.

B2 (Vantage or upper intermediate)

- Can understand the main ideas of complex text on both concrete and abstract topics, including technical discussions in their field of specialization.
- Can interact with a degree of fluency and spontaneity that makes regular interaction with native speakers quite possible without strain for either party.

- Can produce clear, detailed text on a wide range of subjects and explain a viewpoint on a topical issue giving the advantages and disadvantages of various options.[25]

In the case of Arabic language, its individual varieties perform selected communication functions which in other live languages can most often be implemented by one variant (with possible different styles of utterances). Thus, to achieve full communication skills, it is advisable for the student to learn basically two language variants during the course of study, differentiated at the phonological, lexical, syntactic and morphological level. Hence, the first degree curriculum on Arabic philology at Jagiellonian University includes learning practical Arabic language (supplemented with translation exercises, media language classes and literary seminars), learning Arabic grammar in the form of lectures and exercises and – treated as a separate module – learning one of the dialects. Getting familiar with the broadly understood cultural context is facilitated by the subjects such as: history of literature, history of the Arab world, history of Islam, culture of the Arabs, etc.

From many years European glottodidactics has postulated joining the practice of foreign language teaching with the presentation of the realities and culture of the region concerned (the so-called area studies). Now this method gained new value. The presentation of the history, mentality, customs of the country leads not only to a better understanding of our interlocutor. It serves after all to develop what we call "intercultural competence" and what can be defined as "a complex ability to manage oneself in the complicated reality of the multilingual and multi-cultural contemporary world". The main teaching objective is now: "to promote the favourable development of the learner's whole personality and sense of identity in response to the enriching experience of otherness in language and culture". Language didactic is therefore analyzed from the perspective of potential intercultural communication and thus drawing attention to the problem of the so called cultural competences which implies another question: *How to teach?*

2nd half of the 20th and the beginning of the 21st century brought about a new angle of looking at the teaching process and induced a revision of the traditional grammar-translation method for teaching foreign languages. Gradually, as mentioned earlier, such elements as knowledge of realities

---

[25] Global scale – Table 1 (CEFR 3.3): Common Reference levels, available on https://www.coe.int/en/web/common-european-framework-reference-languages/table-1-cefr-3.3-common-reference-levels-global-scale (27.06.2020).

and culture of the countries speaking given language were being included in teaching a foreign language. A cognitive method (factual approach) in the didactics of foreign languages, which assumed integration of such elements as history or higher culture in the teaching process, was replaced with a communicative approach. It assumed that one uses given foreign language just as its native users do. Now, this method is superseded by an intercultural approach.

The changes in the methodical approach can also be observed in didactics of the Arabic language. However, as has been proven by teaching experiments, when it comes to didactics of teaching Arabic, it is not always recommended to base on the most recent teaching methods only. Complex grammar rules of literary Arabic are often better acquired by learners when they are presented in the traditional form and later practiced using e.g. a number of automation enhancing exercises. So often it is the combined approach, which takes advantage of some selected elements of different teaching methods for the completion of specific teaching goals, that turns out to be the most effective.[26]

Iwona Król,[27] the author of the first Polish study addressing the problems of teaching Arabic as a foreign language, is in favour of using a modern communication approach in didactics of modern Arabic,[28] pointing out its eclectic nature,[29] i.e. the possibility of using techniques developed under previous methods, such as audio-lingual method, cognitive-based method or structure-globular method.[30] It should be emphasized that the legally guaranteed autonomy of universities as well as the rights of academic teachers allow for individualised teaching methods, assuming high praxeological competence[31] of didactics (ability to develop own curriculum, operationalisation of general educational goals, construction of own didactic aids).

---

26 E. Machut-Mendecka, *Koncepcje nauczania języka arabskiego*, in: B. Michalak-Pikulska, M. Lewicka (eds.), *Dydaktyka języka arabskiego*, pp. 45–71.

27 I. Król, *Nauczanie języka arabskiego*, Wydawnictwo Uniwersytetu Jagiellońskiego, Kraków 2005.

28 See among others: E. Goldmann (ed.), *Beiträge zur Fachdidaktik Arabisch. Didactische und methodische Probleme des modernen Arabischunterrichts*, Peter Lang, Frankfurt am Main 1993; H.L. Nielsen, *How to Teach Arabic Communicatively: Toward a Theoretical Framework for TAFL*, in: A. Elgibali (ed.), *Understanding Arabic, Essays in Contemporary Arabic Linguistics in Honor of El-Said Badawi*, The American University of Cairo Press, Cairo 1996, pp. 211–239.

29 Ibid., p. 17.

30 See R.M. Rammuny, *Advanced Standard Arabic through Authentic Texts and Audiovisual Materials*, Part 1–2, The University of Michigan Press, Ann Arbor 1994–1996.

31 See K. Denek, *Kompetencje nauczycieli w kontekście wyzwań XXI wieku i potrzeb reformy systemu edukacji w Polsce*, in: K. Wenta (ed.), *Kształcenie pedagogiczne*

2.2. Student perspective

Deliberations about the competences developed in the process of teaching a foreign language lead to another question: *Who do we teach?* or maybe rather: *Whom we would like to educate?* and another important element of the education process, that is the expectations of "the clients" of the teaching process.

Over the last dozen or so years a change in the attitude of potential students to the teaching process to a more pragmatic approach can have been observed. Higher education is no longer perceived as a value in itself, it became just another step in the career path aimed at securing success on the labour market.

At the turn of 2019 and 2020, in December and January, the Students' Council of the Philological Faculty conducted a survey whose purpose was to obtain general information on the popularity of supplementary MA studies at the faculty and to examine the students' attitude to theses. The study covered third-year undergraduate and first-year supplementary master's students.

Among 195 first-degree students participating in the survey, 39 people (20% of respondents) mentioned the lack of possibility to focus the studies on professional work as a reason for not continuing studies, while only 5 people (2.56%) told about no possibility to focus the studies on the scientific work. Out of 160 respondents, 106 supplementary degree students indicated their willingness to deepen their practical knowledge as a reason to study, which is 65.03% of respondents. The 71 respondents declared their willingness to deepen their theoretical knowledge, which is 43.56% of respondents, respectively.

These results clearly prove that students' expectation at this level of education is to acquire the practical knowledge focused on future professional work.

Few years ago, in 2015, in response to a petition filed by the employees in charge of the quality of education, the University's Academic Career Centre carried out a project "Oriental Studies on the Labour Market. Opinion Research Among Employers of Graduates of Oriental Studies". The main aim of the research was to learn the employers' opinion on the competences of graduates of Oriental Studies (diagnosis of desired competences, gaps

---

w dobie przemian edukacyjnych w Polsce. Materiały Konferencyjne nr 46, Wydawnictwo Naukowe Uniwersytetu Szczecińskiego, Szczecin 2000, pp. 29–45.

and competence surplus). The project was in the form of a two module research. The main module of the project, the so-called employers module was based on interviews with employers, so-called mini-depths. There were 20 mini-depths, most of them with HR Managers, Department Managers, recruiters and company owners. The module was supplemented with a desk research which included an analysis of job offers aimed at graduates of Oriental Studies (all specializations offered by the Institute of Oriental Studies within the Neolinguistics Programmes – Oriental Studies, which apart from Arabic Studies also include Turkish Studies, Iranian Studies, Indian Studies, Japanese Studies and Chinese Studies[32]). The desk research contained an analysis of job and internship offers published on the website of the Career Section of the Jagiellonian University between 2011 and 2014. What is especially worth noting is the fact that:

- Over half of all offers did not include the requirement to be a graduate of an institution of higher education, however the adverts included the requirement of fluency in an oriental language combined with a fluent knowledge of English.
- All offers were from the private sector.
- The most frequent specialization among potential employers was financial industry.

The information obtained can prove the previous thesis – it is not the level of education but specific competences that matter on the labour market today. This puts institutions of higher education in the position where they have to compete with other forms of education such as language schools, private lessons with a language teachers or even lessons with native speakers which often have the advantage of reinforcing language competences and communicative behaviours which are useful in face to face communication, or to put it simply – they teach the "real language". Institutions of higher education are therefore forced to face new problems connected with their functioning in a broadly defined market of formal and informal education, which is determined by the notion "success on labour market".

Another important observation was that labour market is not looking for translators, the profession most typically associated with philological education. On the other hand, it is exceptionally absorptive when it comes for specialists in business support sectors with knowledge of foreign language. However, much to our relief, the employers themselves said in the

---

[32] The last one was established in the academic year 2015/2016 and therefore was not taken into consideration in the research.

interviews that it is much easier to train potential employees to perform certain professional, branch related duties that to teach them a language. But is this the only solution?

Every year the number of students completing two fields of study at one time in rising. And usually they are not two philological fields of study. More and more often the first major is Law, Administration or even Medicine. Also the number of students who change their specialization after the first cycle of higher education – undergraduate studies – is going up. In accordance with curricular guidelines, the University is trying to introduce more and more "flexible" programme offer by offering the possibility of selecting subjects which are taught at different departments. But what with those who are already employed and need language teaching that is closely connected with their profession? Can university education also meet their needs?

2.3. "Raising Qualifications of Border Guards and Employees in Intercultural Competencies" project

In the academic year 2011/2012 the Institute of Oriental Studies was a partner-contractor in the project entitled "Raising Qualifications of Border Guards and Employees in Intercultural Competencies" implemented and co-financed within the frames of the European Fund for the Integration of third-country nationals (EFI).[33]

The project consisted in organising a one-year postgraduate programme "Social and Cultural Identity of Middle East Nations" for a group of 30 border guards and employees from the Headquarters of the Karpacki Border Guard Unit and its subordinate units. The studies included culture, history and contemporary social and political issues of Middle East countries. Its integral part was an intense course of selected oriental languages – to be chosen from: Arabic, Turkish, Urdu. The project included approximately 200 hours of theoretical subjects and 120 hours of practical learning of the selected language. It was a part-time course which lasted two semesters. The classes were held at weekends (Friday–Sunday), consisted of 12 meetings and two examination sessions. The language was taught in three language groups. Language classes held during meetings were supplemented by e-learning of oriental language using an internet communicator. The course finished with a diploma exam.

---

[33] In 2011 dr Barbara Ostafin held the position of Head of studies, in 2012 dr Agnieszka Pałka-Lasek.

It must be stressed that the programme was developed specially to meet the requirements and needs of the project. One of the basic assumptions taken into account by our facility, being a philological studies facility, when developing a detailed programme of study were the guidelines for teaching foreign language for specialist purposes. Therefore, three elements, the components of teaching foreign language for specialist purposes, played an important role here. First of all, language teaching designed to develop specific skills, resulting from some specific defined language needs and the need to develop them within a limited time period. Second, consideration of the extra-linguistic aspect (either through contextualization of teaching by means of individual, broader lectures or through emphasis on developing cultural, communicative and pragmatic competencies in language teaching itself). Third, ongoing learning needs analysis enabling introduction of amendments to the teaching content, methods and techniques, but also taking into consideration the learning and teaching potential (like for example any limitations connected with professional duties, consideration of the distance from university to workplace through the introduction of e-learning).

Undoubtedly, the project programme could not be completely free from external conditions, the more prosaic ones such as specific learning requirements including those connected with the programme of study and in particular the final exam, but also more fundamental ones like need to combine teaching language for professional purposes with a basic language course (level A-1, A-2). Therefore, apart from acquisition of specific knowledge, the course was meant to demonstrate tools used to gain and broaden one's knowledge.

The fundamental aim of the project clearly places it among the so called "lifelong learning" activities. The importance of this factor for current academic teaching process can be shown e.g. by the fact it is named to be one of the three reasons for introducing the National Qualifications Framework in Poland.

3. New challenges

The beginning of the 2020s brought new challenges for Polish academic didactics. On the one hand, there was another legal change – in the 2019/2020 academic year – implementation of the Law on Higher Education and

Science, so called "Constitution" for education.[34] This comprehensive reform of higher education, modifying the concept of scientific disciplines, resulted not only in numerous procedural and organizational changes, but also a requirement to modify curricula. However, the key here seems to be the admission of the Jagiellonian University to the so-called research universities, selected as part of the Ministry of Science's competition "Initiative of Excellence" (IDUB) – the list of 10 universities that will become flagship research centers in Poland. In this light, it seems that the scientific context of language education is strengthening, which can distinguish the university-level education from various forms of "commercial" education.

At the same time, environmental opposition raises the need to enter oriental studies (like other philologies, which are essentially an interdisciplinary field) into a rigid concept of dividing disciplines into linguistics and literary studies. It is worth mentioning that in Poland for many years (among others on the part of University of Warsaw) the efforts are being made to recognize Orientalism as a separate scientific discipline within the humanities, which would make it possible to confer doctoral and postdoctoral degrees in the Oriental studies.

The year 2020 also brought a sudden and unexpected change in teaching methods, forcing a rapid entry into the age of distance education, which until now in Poland, in the case of didactics of the Arabic language, was rather the domain of private lessons, implementing online courses. However, this sphere requires a lot of coordinated activities from the university departments, starting from the introduction of subsequent normative regulations by adjusting technical infrastructure, modifying programmes, developing scientific aids and launching teaching support. Nevertheless, it opens up many new opportunities and, above all, is becoming an increasingly indispensable platform for communication with the young generation.

And still the last basic question remains: *How to reconcile the mission of institutions of higher education with the pragmatic market needs and the current "consumer" needs with the guidelines for central curricula? Is such a compromise possible?*

Probably, there is no one ready formula. Nevertheless, some clues seem to be important from the point of view of increasing the quality of teaching.

---

34 See provisions of the act Ustawa z dnia 20 lipca 2018 r. – Prawo o szkolnictwie wyższym i nauce (Dz.U. z 2018 r., poz. 1668). See also Ustawa z dnia 3 lipca 2018 r. – Przepisy wprowadzające ustawę – Prawo o szkolnictwie wyższym i nauce (Dz.U. z 2018 r., poz. 1669).

They constitute, to a certain degree (at least when it comes to the programmes and teaching methods), an amplification of the previously mentioned guidelines for the Arabic language teaching curriculum for students of Arabic Studies developed by Professor Elżbieta Górska and Marek Skoczek:[35]

- Ongoing verification and improvement of curricula including different forms of communication and language level and taking into consideration the number of language phenomena in order to make students familiar with the complexity of the socio-linguistic situation of the Arabic speaking countries, and hence.
- Making reference between specific speech situations and appropriate language forms. This includes ongoing monitoring of language development and being sensitive to any changes in language standards.
- Basing teaching materials on authentic materials to a maximum possible extent.
- Developing all communication competencies, including language, cultural and social competencies, that is not possible without direct contact with the language. Hence the important role of student and staff exchange programme and extremely valuable for us opportunity to learn and to benefit from the rich experience of our partner universities and research centres in Arab countries.
- Taking into account the need for lifelong learning (cooperation with other sectors aimed at completion of joint partner projects).
- Taking into consideration student needs, also through graduate tracer studies and labour market research as well as intensifying cooperation with companies and institutions which can help introduce students to labour market.
- Studying the possibility of making educational offer more flexible, so that it can be adjusted to more individual student needs or the needs of a group of students.
- Developing interdisciplinary projects and programmes.

The last two points promote cooperation between units within one institution of higher education, but also cooperation between institutions of higher education on national and international level with the aim of creating joint educational programmes which would become a long-term educational offer.[36]

---

[35] E. Górska, M. Skoczek, A. Hasan, *Dydaktyka języka arabskiego*, pp. 14–25.

[36] Several "mixed programs" have already been implemented at Polish universities, e.g. English Studies with Arabic at Silesia University in Katowice and Kazimierz

However despite the orientation of language teaching on practical skills, one should agree with the postulate[37] that this teaching at the academic level never cannot take place in isolation from the scientific context.

References

Abboud P.F., *The Teaching of Arabic in the United States. The State of the Art*, Center for Applied Linguistics, Washington, DC 1968.

Badawi El-Said M., *Educated Spoken Arabic: A Problem in Teaching Arabic as a Foreign Language*, in: K. Jankowsky (ed.), *Scientific and Humanistic Dimensions of Language* (pp. 15–22), John Benjamins, Amsterdam–Philadelphia, 1985.

Blanc Ch., *Style Variations in Spoken Arabic: A Sample of Interdialectical Educated Conversation*, in: A.Ch. Ferguson at al. (eds.), *Contribution to Arabic Linguistics* (pp. 81–158), Harvard University Press, Cambridge 1960.

Blau J., *Studies in Middle Arabic and Its Judaeo-Arabic Variety*, Magnes Press, Jerusalem 1988.

Danecki J., *Gramatyka języka arabskiego*, Wydawnictwo Akademickie Dialog, Warszawa 1994.

Danecki J., *Współczesny język arabski i jego dialekty*, Wydawnictwo Akademickie Dialog, Warszawa 2000.

Denek K., *Kompetencje nauczycieli w kontekście wyzwań XXI wieku i potrzeb reformy systemu edukacji w Polsce*, in: K. Wenta (ed.), *Kształcenie pedagogiczne w dobie przemian edukacyjnych w Polsce. Materiały Konferencyjne nr 46* (pp. 29–45), Wydawnictwo Naukowe Uniwersytetu Szczecińskiego, Szczecin 2000.

Ferguson Ch., *Diglossia*, "Word" 1959, 15, pp. 325–340.

Goldmann E. (ed.), *Beiträge zur Fachdidaktik Arabisch. Didactische und methodische Probleme des modernen Arabischunterrichts*, Peter Lang, Frankfurt am Main 1993.

Górska E., *Wybrane zagadnienia dydaktyki uniwersyteckiej języka arabskiego*, "Biuletyn Glottodydaktyczny" (Kraków) 2003, 9–10, pp. 135–140.

Górska E., Skoczek M., Hasan A., *Dydaktyka języka arabskiego*, Wydawnictwo Akademickie Dialog, Warszawa 1999.

Hamilton A., *Arabic Studies in Europe*, in: K. Versteeg, *Encyclopedia of Arabic Language and Linguistics*, V (pp. 166–172), E.J. Brill, Leiden 2011.

Wielki University in Bydgoszcz as well as French Arabic Programme at Mikołaj Kopernik University in Toruń.

[37] J. Łacina, *Kulturowo-techniczne problemy...*, p. 34.

Król I., *Nauczanie języka arabskiego*, Wydawnictwo Uniwersytetu Jagiellońskiego, Kraków 2005.

Łacina J., *Kulturowo-techniczne problemy dydaktyki języka arabskiego na początku XXI wieku – nowe wyzwania*, in: B. Michalak-Pikulska, M. Lewicka (eds.), *Dydaktyka języka arabskiego* (pp. 29–43), Wydawnictwo Naukowe Uniwersytetu Mikołaja Kopernika, Toruń 2013.

Machut-Mendecka E., *Koncepcje nauczania języka arabskiego*, in: B. Michalak-Pikulska, M. Lewicka (eds.), *Dydaktyka języka arabskiego* (pp. 45–71), Wydawnictwo Naukowe Uniwersytetu Mikołaja Kopernika, Toruń 2013.

Marçais W., *La diglossie arabe*, "L'enseigment public" 1930, 97, pp. 401–409.

Michalak-Pikulska B., *Studia arabistyczne w Krakowie*, in: L. Sudyka (ed.), *Orientalia Commemorativa* (pp. 43–48), Wydawnictwo Uniwersytetu Jagiellońskiego, Kraków 2011.

Mitchell T.F., *The Teaching of Arabic in Great Britain, Linguistic Report*, "Newsletter of the Center for Applied Linguistics" (Washington) 1969, 11/2 (April), Suppl. 20.

Nalborczyk A.S., *Zachowania językowe imigrantów arabskich w Austrii*, Wydawnictwo Akademickie Dialog, Warszawa 2003.

Nielsen H.L., *How to Teach Arabic Communicatively: Toward a Theoretical Framework for TAFL*, in: A. Elgibali (ed.), *Understanding Arabic, Essays in Contemporary Arabic Linguistics in Honor of El-Said Badawi* (pp. 211–239), The American University of Cairo Press, Cairo 1996.

Paraskiewicz K., *Orientaliści krakowscy*, in: L. Sudyka (ed.), *Orientalia Commemorativa* (pp. 75–88), Wydawnictwo Uniwersytetu Jagiellońskiego, Kraków 2011.

Paraskiewicz K., *Z historii orientalistyki w Uniwersytecie Jagiellońskim*, in: J. Świt (ed.), *Języki i cywilizacje* (pp. 15–34), Wydział Filologiczny Uniwersytetu Jagiellońskiego – Wydawnictwo Nowa Strona, Kraków–Bielsko-Biała 2019.

Parzymies A., *L'enseignement de l'arabe littéral face à la diglossie*, in: R.T. Nasr (ed.), *The Teaching of Arabic to Adults in Europe (Proceedings of the 14th AIMAV Seminar, 23–25 May 1983, Collection d' Études Linguistiques*, 32) (pp. 29–35), AIMAV, Bruxelles 1983.

Pilsztynowa S., *Proceder podróży i życia mego awantur*, Wydawnictwo Literackie, Kraków 1957.

Pisowicz A., *Stulecie krakowskiej orientalistyki*, in: J. Świt (ed.), *Języki i cywilizacje* (pp. 7–13), Wydział Filologiczny Uniwersytetu Jagiellońskiego – Wydawnictwo Nowa Strona, Kraków–Bielsko-Biała 2019.

Potocki J., *Voyage en Turquie et en Egypte fait en 1784*, Warszawa 1788.

Potocki J., *Voyage dans l'Empire de Maroc, fait en l'année 1791. Suivi du Voyage de Hafez, récit oriental*, Warszawa 1792.

Rammuny R.M., *Advanced Standard Arabic through Authentic Texts and Audiovisual Materials*, Part 1–2, The University of Michigan Press, Ann Arbor 1994–1996.

Al-Sayadi M., *Język literacki oraz dialekty w dydaktyce języka arabskiego. Kayfa ḥāluka czy keyf ḥālek?*, in: B. Michalak-Pikulska, M. Lewicka (eds.), *Dydaktyka języka arabskiego* (pp. 197–207), Wydawnictwo Naukowe Uniwersytetu Mikołaja Kopernika, Toruń 2013.

Tapiero N. (1976), *Pour une didatique de l'arabe moderne, langue de communication: problématique et solution*, v. I–II, Lille–Paris.

Legal acts

Global scale – Table 1 (CEFR 3.3): Common Reference levels, https://www.coe.int/en/web/common-european-framework-reference-languages/table-1-cefr-3.3-common-reference-levels-global-scale (27.06.2020).

Council of Europe, Common European Framework of Reference for Languages: Learning, Teaching, Assessment, 2011.

Ustawa z dnia 18 marca 2011 r. o zmianie ustawy – Prawo o szkolnictwie wyższym, ustawy o stopniach naukowych i tytule naukowym oraz o stopniach i tytule w zakresie sztuki oraz o zmianie niektórych innych ustaw (Dz.U. z 2011 r. Nr 84, poz. 455).

Ustawa z dnia 3 lipca 2018 r. – Przepisy wprowadzające ustawę – Prawo o szkolnictwie wyższym i nauce (Dz.U. z 2018 r., poz. 1669).

Ustawa z dnia 20 lipca 2018 r. – Prawo o szkolnictwie wyższym i nauce (Dz.U. z 2018 r., poz. 1668).

IWONA KRÓL

Meanings and functions of genitive constructions in Modern Standard Arabic

In Arabic and in other Semitic languages[1] a substantive (standing in the genitive case) may occur as *nomen rectum*[2] i.e. as genitival qualifier that determines another substantive, which precedes it and stands in the construct state (*status constructus*). Some substantives – as well as adjectives and numerals – if occur as *nomen regens* in genitive constructions, on account of their semantic properties require (as *nomen rectum*) substantives having particular grammatical properties. The form of a genitive qualifier determines then the meaning of the determined noun and of the whole phrase.

In this paper I am going to investigate, how the form of a qualifier (its definiteness vs. indefiniteness and number) differentiates meanings of such constructions as well as of their heads.

There are numerous studies on genitive constructions and in most cases they constitute parts of monographs on the entire system of Arabic language or its syntax. Among them there are titles quoted in this paper: J. Danecki (2001), El-Said Badawi, M.G. Carter, A. Gully (2004), R. Buckley (2004), C. Holes (2004), K.C. Ryding (2005). Usually they focus on

---

1 E. Lipiński, *Semitic Languages Outline of a Comparative Grammar*, Peeters, Leuven 1997, p. 497.

2 Arabic term: الْمُضَافُ إِلَيْهِ, see K. Versteegh (ed.), *Encyclopedia of Arabic Language and Linguistics*, Vol. 2, Brill, Leiden–Boston 2006–2009, p. 294.

lexemes appearing as *nomen regens* and analyse their syntactic and semantic functions.

Aims of this paper are: (i) to group genitive constructions according to the grammatical form of a qualifier; (ii) to indicate how the elements of meaning present throughout such groups depend on the form of a qualifier.

Below I present a list of possible models of that construction, in which in the position of genitival qualifier there occur indefinite or definite nouns. The examples[3] I present, are divided into three groups according to the grammatical form of the qualifiers, which can be: (i) indefinite nouns, (ii) definite nouns. Then for comparison: (iii) indefinite or definite nouns in cases when definiteness or indefiniteness of the qualifier does not affect the meaning of the whole phrase. In conclusion I indicate semantic consequences of particular combinations. Numerous examples are intended to show various possible contexts, in which particular qualifier may occur, and to highlight differences in meaning resulting from various grammatical forms of qualifiers.

In the analyzed phrases as the determined nouns (*nomen regens*)[4] there occur substantives, adjectives or numerals.[5] The case in which determined noun stands, depends on the syntactic function of the whole phrase. A noun which occurs in this position has no prepositive definite article nor nunation.[6] As *nomen regens* there sometimes occur proper names.[7]

مِصْرُ: مِصْرُ المُسْتَقْبَلِ

Egypt of the future (Al-Ahrām, 5.04.2011)

If in other contexts they occur with definite articles, in such constructions they lose them.

السُّودَانُ: سُودَانُ الغَدِ

Tomorrow's Sudan [Sudan of tomorrow] (Al-Waṭan, 30.04.2011)

---

3 The presented examples come from several contemporary Arabic novels, as well as from the Internet editions of the Arabic newspapers. The examples are mostly presented in sentence contexts. Arabic texts are vocalized so as to highlight the internal syntactical relations within the sentences.

4 Arabic term: المُضَاف, see K. Versteegh (ed.), *Encyclopedia...*, p. 294.

5 E. Lipiński, *Semitic Languages...*, p. 497.

6 K. Versteegh (ed.), *Encyclopedia...*, p. 296.

7 El-Said Badawi, M.G. Carter, A. Gully, *Modern Written Arabic: A Comprehensive Grammar*, Routledge, London–New York 2004, p. 134.

Only when as *nomen regens* there occur an adjective having syntactic function of adjectival attribute of a definite substantive,[8] it may be preceded by a definite article.[9]

فِي جَانِبٍ آخَرَ مِنْ رَصِيفِ شَارِعِ الحَمْرَاءِ الدِّمَشْقِيِّ يَتَوَقَّفُ بَائِعُ الكَسْتَنَاءِ، تِلْكَ الثِّمَارِ اللَّذِيذِ الطَّعْمِ.

On the other side of the Al-Ḥamrā' street in Damascus there stops a seller of chestnuts – fruits delicious to the taste. (Aš-Šarq al-Awsaṭ, 12.03.2011)

جَمِيعُهَا فِي السَّرَاةِ المُمْتَدَّةِ مِنْ حُدُودِ مُحَافَظَةِ الطَّائِفِ غَرْباً إِلَى حُدُودِ عَسِيرَ تُلَوِّنُهَا الأَشْجَارُ الدَّائِمَةُ الخَضْرَةِ.

They are all on the hill stretching out from the boundary of the province of Aṭ-Ṭā'if in the west to the boundary of the province of 'Asīr, which are added some colour by the evergreen trees [lit. trees permanent of green]. (Aš-Šarq al-Awsaṭ, 27.05.2011)

Genitive constructions are definite if and only if *nomen rectum* is a definite substantive.[10] The occurrence of an indefinite *nomen rectum* results in indefiniteness of the whole phrase.[11] It can be easily demonstrated, when we supplement such a construction with an adjective – definite and indefinite one. What we get is:

a) a nominal phrase:

خَمْسَةُ وُزَرَاءِ خَارِجِيَّةٍ عَرَبٍ

Five Arab foreign ministers (Aš-Šarq al-Awsaṭ: 22.03.2011)

According to the syntax of agreement the indefinite adjective (in the above example) is an attribute of an indefinite noun phrase.

يَتَبَنَّي وُزَرَاءُ الخَارِجِيَّةِ العَرَبُ قَرَارًا.

Arab foreign ministers will pass the resolution. (Al-Ahrām: 13.03.2011)

---

8 "Adjectival iḍāfa" – see: R. Buckley, *Modern Literary Arabic. A Reference Grammar*, Librairie du Liban Publ., Beirut 2004, p. 175.

9 El-Said Badawi, M.G. Carter, A. Gully, *Modern Written Arabic...*, p. 131; E. Lipiński, *Semitic Languages...*, p. 499.

10 R. Buckley, *Modern Literary Arabic...*, p. 156; C. Holes, *Modern Arabic. Structures, Functions, and Varieties*, revised edition, Georgetown University Press, Washington 2004, p. 200.

11 R. Buckley, *Modern Literary Arabic...*, p. 156; E. Lipiński, *Semitic Languages...*, pp. 501–502.

In the above phrase the adjective is a definite one because it is an attribute of a definite noun phrase (with a definite *nomen rectum*).

b) or a nominal sentence:

غُرَفُ النَّوْمِ مَفْصُولَةٌ.

Bedrooms are separate. (Al-Maḥādīn 2003, p. 273)

In the above phrase the definite noun phrase supplemented with the indefinite adjective results in nominal sentence.

In a genitive construction a postpositive qualifier immediately follows *nomen regens* and stands in the genitive case.[12] However semantic relations between them vary from case to case. The centre of meaning of such a nominal phrase it may be:

- its head (determined noun), e.g.

يُحَضَّرُ الفُولُ المَسْلُوقُ مَعَ البَنَدُورَةِ الخَضْرَاءِ والبَقْدُونِسِ مَعَ عَصِيرِ اللَّيْمُونِ.

Cooked broad beans are prepared with green tomatoes and parsley with the addition of some lemon juice. (Aš-Šarq al-Awsaṭ, 12.03.2011)

- or genitive qualifier, e.g.

نَحْصُلُ عَلَى دَرَجَاتٍ مُرْتَفِعَةٍ فِي كُلِّ المَوَادِّ.

We get good marks in all subjects. (Aš-Šarq al-Awsaṭ, 30.10.2011)

Some substantives, adjectives and numerals, that occur in such constructions as *nomen regens*, formally are determined words (as in the last example above), but it is words occurring as *nomen rectum* that are semantically more significant. Meanings of such phrases often depend on the grammatical form of *nomen rectum* (its definiteness or inefiniteness and its number). Below I present a list of possible models of such a construction. I begin with phrases in which as genitive qualifiers there occur (obligatorily) indefinite substantives.

12 E. Lipiński, *Semitic Languages*..., p. 502.

I. Indefinite substantive as a genitive qualifier (*nomen rectum*)

Phrases with indefinite substantive as a genitive qualifier are themselves indefinite ones.

حَضَرَ الشَّيْخُ لأَوَّلِ مَرَّةٍ فِي المَجْلِسِ.

Sheikh has participated in the council meeting for the first time. (Al-Maḥādīn, 78)

فِي حَفْلَةِ العَيْدِ الَّتِي أُقِيمَتْ لِأَوَّلِ مَرَةٍ فِي التَّاسِعِ مِنْ شَهْرِ دِيسَمْبَرَ.

During the holiday celebration, which for the first time was organized on the 9th of December. (Al-Maḥādīn, 476)

In contexts that demand definite phrases different syntactic structures are being used: postpositive numerals or adjectives stand in agreement relation with the definite substantives determined by them.

وَهِىَ المَرَّةُ الأُولَى الَّتِى تُمَثَّلُ فِيهَا الرِّوَايَةُ بِالكَامِلِ مِنْ قِبَلِ طُلاَّبِ المَدْرَسَةِ.

It was the first time when the whole novel was staged by the students. (Al-Maḥādīn, 214)

كَانَتْ تِلْكَ هِىَ المَرَّةَ الأُولَى.

This was the first time. (Šuqayr, 120)

I. a) Indefinite singular substantive as a genitive qualifier

- **Substantive كُلٌّ (meaning: every, each [lit. whole])**[13]

Indefinite singular substantive occurs as a determiner when the substantive كُلّ, is to point out every element of some set. The postpositioned substantive is a centre of meaning of such a phrase. It can be easily seen in the way the gender congruence between the whole phrase and the other components of the sentence is being accomplished:

كُنْتُ حَرِيصَةً أَنْ تَعْرِفَ كُلُّ طَالِبَةٍ بَلَدَهَا الأَصْلِيَّ.

I desired every student (female) to know her home country. (Al-Kayyālī, 90)

---

13 El-Said Badawi, M.G. Carter, A. Gully, *Modern Written Arabic...*, p. 224; R. Buckley, *Modern Literary Arabic...*, p. 184; J. Danecki, *Gramatyka języka arabskiego*, Vol. 2, Wydawnictwo Akademickie Dialog, Warszawa 2001, p. 53.

In the above example the predicate of the subordinate sentence is grammatically accommodated to *nomen rectum* (feminine gender).

This principle covers also the cases, when such word groups are being substituted with equivalent pronouns:

كُنْتُ أعِيشُ مَعَ كُلِّ طَالِبَةٍ أشْعُرُ أنَّهَا بِحَاجَةٍ لِي.

I stayed with every [female] student that I felt, [she] needed me. (Al-Maḥādīn, 90)

The pronoun that substitutes word group is feminine – just like the genitive qualifier.

So the prepositioned substantive governs the substantive determining it and the latter must stand in the genitive case, whereas the way the agreement relation between the whole phrase and the other components of the sentence is being accomplished, depends on the meaning of the phrase.

- **Numerals hundred (مِئَةٌ), thousand (أَلْفٌ), million (مِلْيُونٌ), billion (مِلْيَارٌ) etc.**[14]

Numerals of this type are distinguished by following syntactic rules of a substantive. In phrases they occur within, they are followed by the counted substantives standing in singular genitive. The syntactic relations of such groups within sentences depend on their meanings. If they are sentence subjects, then predicates – only when following them, e.g. in some object clauses or clauses with marked word orders – are grammatically accommodated to them, which includes plurality and the personal – impersonal differentiation:

460 ألفَ شَابٍّ مِصْرِيٍّ هَاجَرُوا لِلإتِّحَادِ الأُورُوبِيِّ خِلاَلَ 10 سَنَوَاتٍ.

460 thousand of young Egyptians have emigrated to the European Union countries during the last decade. (Al-Ahrām, 10.04.2010)

The phrase 460 ألفَ شَابٍّ مِصْرِيٍّ, in which both the numeral "thousand" and the substantive are grammatically singular, has a meaning of a plural personal substantive (الشَّبَابُ "young people") and results in appropriate syntax of the whole sentence.

---

[14] El-Said Badawi, M.G. Carter, A. Gully, *Modern Written Arabic*..., pp. 264–268; R. Buckley, *Modern Literary Arabic*..., pp. 919–923.

- **Elative adjectives (أَفْعَل) used for a superlative[15]**

They are used (always masculine) as *nomen rectum* in phrases in which they are followed by indefinite singular substantives.

كَانَتْ تِلْكَ أَجْمَلَ ذِكْرَى أَحْمِلُهَا مَعِي مِنْ هُنَاكَ.

It was the most beautiful reminiscence I had gained there. (Šuqayr, 239)

أَرْجُو التَّكَرُّمَ بِإِرْسَالِ الطَّالِبَيْنِ فِي أَسْرَعِ وَقْتٍ مُمْكِنٍ.

I would be grateful, if you could send the students as soon as possible [lit. within the shortest time possible]. (Al-Maḥādīn, 486)

- **Ordinal numeral أَوَّلُ ("first")[16]**

This numeral is a suppletive form of the cardinal numeral وَاحِدٌ ("one").[17] These words have different roots, and the numeral أَوَّلُ ("first") is built according to the word pattern of an elative (أَفْعَل). There is also a similarity of meanings: أَوَّلُ means also "the most exposed", "the most prominent" etc. Phrases with أَوَّلُ as their heads are built in a similar way as phrases with elatives. The numeral is masculine, just as are elatives in comparable constructions.

أَذْكُرُ أَنَّ أَوَّلَ قَصِيدَةٍ كَانَتْ بِمُنَاسَبَةِ اسْتِشْهَادِ الضَّابِطِ.

I remember, that the first poem was devoted to martyrdom of the officer. (Al-Kayyālī, 80)

وَاخْتَرْتُ أَعْمَالًا لِأُشَاكِّلَ مِنْهَا أَوَّلَ مُحَاوَلَةٍ شِعْرِيَّةٍ لِلنَّشْرِ.

I have selected works for my first poetic publication [lit. the first poetic attempt in print]. (Al-Kayyālī, 143)

وَأَذْكُرُ أَنَّنِي أَمْسَكْتُ بِيَدِ أُمِّي لأُشَارِكَ فِي أَوَّلِ مَسِيرَةٍ شَعْبِيَّةٍ وَطَنِيَّةٍ.

I remember, I took my mother by the hand, in order to take part in the first popular-national demonstration. (Al-Kayyālī, 16)

---

15 El-Said Badawi, M.G. Carter, A. Gully, *Modern Written Arabic...*, p. 251; R. Buckley, *Modern Literary Arabic...*, pp. 641–643.

16 El-Said Badawi, M.G. Carter, A. Gully, *Modern Written Arabic...*, p. 271; R. Buckley, *Modern Literary Arabic...*, p. 936.

17 In other Semitic languages there is a similar situation: E. Lipiński, *Semitic Languages...*, p. 293.

كُنْتُ مَعَ أَوَّلِ وَفْدٍ أُرْدُنِيٍّ فِلَسْطِينِيٍّ

I was [there] together with the first Jordanian-Palestinian delegation. (Al-Kayyālī 2005, 156)

اسْتَلَمْتُ أَوَّلَ رَاتِبٍ.

I got my first salary. (Al-Kayyālī, 87)

أَوَّلُ سَوْدَاءَ حَازَتْ عَلَى الجَائِزَةِ.

The first black woman, who got the prize. (Aš-Šarq al-Awsaṭ, 9.01.2011)

- **Other ordinal numerals: second (ثَانٍ), third (ثَالِثٌ), etc.**

They are built according to a pattern of فَاعِلٌ on a basis of 3-consonant roots of cardinal numerals. The root of the numeral ثَامِنٌ ("eighth") is reduced: in order to obtain demanded 3-consonant root, the consonant *-y-* is removed. From a synchronical point of view the form of the numeral سَادِسٌ ("sixth") is a suppletive form of the cardinal numeral سِتٌّ ("six"). Phrases including these numerals are built identically to the phrases including the numeral أَوَّلُ and elatives mentioned above.

فِي ثَانِي يَوْمٍ مِنَ الزِّيَارَةِ.

On the second day of the visit (Al-Maḥādīn, 79)

ثَالِثُ بَيْتٍ هُوَ بَيْتُكُمْ.

The third house it is your house. (Al-Kayyālī, 122)

دَعْمُ الأَزْهَرِ لِلْفُنُونِ جَعَلَ مِنَ السِّينَمَا المِصْرِيَّةِ رَابِعَ أَكْبَرِ صِنَاعَةِ فِيلْمٍ فِي العَالَمِ.

The support of Al-Azhar for the arts made Egiptian cinematography the world's fourth largest film industry. (Aš-Šarq al-Awsaṭ, 9.04.2011)

In contexts that demand definite phrases there occur syntactic structures consisting of definite substantives (as their heads) and of definite ordinal numerals as adjectival attributes standing in agreement relation.[18]

وَصَلُوا إِلَى البَحْرَيْنِ فِي الأُسْبُوعِ الأَوَّلِ.

They came to Bahrain in the first week. (Al-Maḥādīn, 212)

[18] El-Said Badawi, M.G. Carter, A. Gully, *Modern Written Arabic*..., p. 271.

انْتَهَتْ الزِّيَارَةُ الأُولَى.

The first visit has finished. (Al-Kayyālī, 117)

- **Adjective آخِرٌ ("last"):**

This adjective (masculine) occurs exclusively in the government relation with substantive in genitive. This phrase is indefinite.

لآخِرِ مَرَّةٍ

For the last time (Al-Kayyālī, 159)

حَتَّى آخِرِ يَوْمٍ

Until the last day (Al-Maḥādīn, 556)

In phrases, in which the adjective „last" functions as an adjectival attribute, there occurs other lexeme: أَخِيرٌ (both with definite and indefinite substantives).

يُعْطَى الرَّئِيسَ فُرْصَةً أَخِيرَةً.

The president is being given a final chance. (Aš-Šarq al-Awsaṭ, 24.02.2011)

ذَلِكَ سَيَكُونُ الخِيَارَ الأَخِيرَ.

It will be the last choice. (Aš-Šarq al-Awsaṭ, 1.01.2011)

I. b) Indefinite plural substantive as a genitive qualifier

- **substantive عِدَّةٌ ("a number"):**

This substantive is used in the context of countable substantives (phrase meaning: "a number of objects", "some objects", "many objects", "a few objects").[19]

جَرَتْ عِدَّةُ مُحَاوَلاتٍ.

There have been some attempts. (Al-Kayyālī, 91)

أَلْقَى عِدَّةَ مُحَاضَرَاتٍ.

He gave a few lectures. (Al-Maḥādīn, 262)

[19] R. Buckley, *Modern Literary Arabic...*, pp. 931–932.

البَيْتُ مُكَوَّنٌ مِنْ عِدَّةِ غُرَفٍ.

The house consists of a few rooms. (Šuqayr, 32)

If the second component of the phrase has to be definite, the genitive attribute can be replaced with prepositional phrase.

أُقِيمَتْ حَفْلَةٌ لِافْتِتَاحِهَا قَامَ بِهَا عِدَّةٌ مِنَ الخُطَبَاءِ [خُطَبَاءِ المَدْرَسَةِ].

There has been given an inaugural reception, organized by a few lecturers [of the school]. (Al-Maḥādīn, 125)

When the genitival qualifier is to be determined by another substantive, the substantive is preceded by preposition:

جُعِلَتْ عِدَّةُ أَنْوَاعٍ مِنْ هذِهِ المَدَارِسِ مَدَارِسَ تَحْضِيرِيَّةً مُسْتَقِلَّةً.

Some of those schools were made independent preparatory schools. (Al-Maḥādīn, 292)

Phrases with the substantive عِدَّةٌ as *nomen regens* are semantically equivalent to the phrases with the same substantive (postpositive, standing in the agreement relation) as apposition. Also in this case both components of the phrase are indefinite.

أَنَا أُحَاوِلُ اصْطِيَادَ عَصْفُورَيْنِ أَوْ عَصَافِيرَ عِدَّةً بِحَجَرٍ وَاحِدٍ.

I am trying to kill two birds or a few birds with one stone. (Šuqayr, 21)

عَسْكَرُوا عَلَى شَاطِئِ البَحْرِ فِي أَمَاكِنَ عِدَّةٍ.

They were camping at a few places at the seaside. (Al-Maḥādīn, 250)

- **Numerals 3–10**[20]

Those numerals stand to substantives in the government relation: the postpositive (indefinite) substantives stand in plural genitive, while numerals occur with the morphem *-at^un^* when they are followed by masculine substantives or without it when they are followed by feminine substantives.

[20] El-Said Badawi, M.G. Carter, A. Gully, *Modern Written Arabic...*, pp. 260–261; R. Buckley, *Modern Literary Arabic...*, pp. 914–916; E. Górska, *Studium kontrastywne składni arabskich i polskich współczesnych tekstów literackich*, Wydawnictwo Uniwersytetu Jagiellońskiego, Kraków 2000, p. 33.

تَمَّ اسْتِقْدَامُ خَمْسَةِ فِلَسْطِينِيِّينَ وَسَبْعَةِ لُبْنَانِيِّينَ.

There were recruited five Palestinians and seven Lebanese. (Al-Maḥādīn, 258)

عَرَفْتُ مِنْهُ أَنَّهُ يُقِيمُ هُنَا مُنْذُ عَشْرِ سَنَوَاتٍ.

I have learned from him, that he has been living here for 10 years. (Šuqayr, 124)

If substantive in such a phrase is to be definite, it is preceded by a preposition:

أُعْطِيَ خَمْسَةٌ مِنَ الذُّكُورِ مِنَحًا دِرَاسِيَّةً.

Five of the men were awarded scholarships. (Al-Maḥādīn, 258)

If the whole phrase is to be definite, the numerals 3–10 follow the definite substantives, standing to them in the agreement relation (as appositions). In this case also the numerals occur with the morphem *-at^{un}* when they follow masculine substantives or without it when they follow feminine substantives.

أَطْفَالُهَا الخَمْسَةُ، طَلَبَاتُهُمْ وَوَاجِبَاتُهُمْ!

Her five children, their demands and responsibilities! (Nāṣir, 48)

وَدَّعْنَا أَفْرَادَ الأُسَرِ الأَرْبَعِ.

We saw the members of those four families off. (Šuqayr, 263)

- **Quantifier بِضْعَةٌ \ بِضْعٌ ("some", "a few", "several")[21]**

Similarly to numerals 3–10, it is followed by an indefinite substantive standing in plural genitive; it occurs with the morphem *-at^{un}* when is followed by a masculine substantive or without it when is followed by a feminine substantive. It indicates a set of 3–10 objects.

بَعْدَ أَنْ وَصَلَتْنِي بِضْعُ بَرْقِيَّاتٍ.

After I had got a few telegrammes. (Al-Maḥādīn, 81)

شَاهَدْتُ بِضْعَةَ بُيُوتٍ قَدِيمَةٍ.

I have seen a few old houses. (Šuqayr, 30)

21 El-Said Badawi, M.G. Carter, A. Gully, *Modern Written Arabic...*, p. 229; R. Buckley, *Modern Literary Arabic...*, p. 931.

I. c) Indefinite singular, dual or plural substantive as a genitive qualifier

- **Participle مُجَرَّدٌ ("mere", "sheer")[22]**

It is followed by singular, dual or plural substantives. It is translated as "only", "solely", "nothing but". The substantive occurring as *nomen rectum* is formally a subordinate component, but it is a centre of meaning of such a phrase.

هِيَ مُجَرَّدُ طِفْلَةٍ مُزْعِجَةٍ.

She is only an annoying child. (Nāṣir, 12)

هَلْ كَانَتْ صُوَرًا حَقِيقِيَّةً أَمْ مُجَرَّدَ أَحْلَامٍ.

Were they true images or only dreams? (Al-ʻAtīq, 49)

هؤُلَاءِ الزُّوَّارُ الذِينَ يَزُورُونَ إِسْبَانِيَا لِمُدَّةِ ثَلَاثَةِ أَيَّامٍ أَكْثَرُ مِنْ مُجَرَّدِ ضُيُوفٍ.

Those visitors, who tour around Spain for three days, are something more than mere guests. (Aš-Šarq al-Awsaṭ, 28.04.2011)

هَلْ كَانَ مُجَرَّدَ مُدَرِّسٍ؟

Was he only a teacher? (Al-Maḥādīn, 33)

لَمْ يَكُنْ الغِنَاءُ حُلْمَهَا إِذَنْ بَلْ مُجَرَّدَ وَسِيلَةٍ لِتَحْقِيقِ حُلْمٍ آخَرَ.

So, singing was not her dream, but only a means for fulfilling another dream. (Nāṣir, 51–52)

رَأَتْ أَنَّ مُجَرَّدَ عَوْدَتِهَا إِلَى العَمَلِ فِي لُبْنَانَ جَعَلَ فَرْحَتَهَا تَكْتَمِلُ.

She realised, that only her return to work in Lebanon had made her joy complete. (Aš-Šarq al-Awsaṭ, 1.04.2011)

- **Indefinite pronoun أَيَّةٌ – أَيٌّ ("any", "whichever"; within negative sentences: "none", "no")[23]**

The most often it occurs as masculine (أَيٌّ) when followed both by masculine and feminine substantives.

22 El-Said Badawi, M.G. Carter, A. Gully, *Modern Written Arabic*..., p. 222.
23 Ibid., pp. 229–230.

يُحْظَرُ عَلَى الْمُوَظَّفِينَ الِانْتِمَاءُ لِأَيِّ حِزْبٍ أَوِ الْمُشَارَكَةُ بِأَيِّ نَشَاطٍ سِيَاسِيٍّ.

Employees are forbidden to belong to any party or to participate in any political activities. (Al-Kayyālī, 91)

لَيْسَ هُنَاكَ أَيُّ دَلِيلٍ.

There is no evidence. (Al-Maḥādīn, 493)

لِأَنَّهَا لَمْ تَكُنْ تَخْضَعُ لِأَيِّ رَقَابَةٍ مِنْ أَيِّ جِهَةٍ.

Because she is not subject to any supervision, by anyone. (Al-Maḥādīn, 530)

لَا تَتَذَكَّرُ أَنَّ وَجْهَ أُمِّهَا قَدْ أَشْرَقَ قَطُّ بِالسَّعَادَةِ فِى أَيِّ لَحَظَاتٍ أُخْرَى.

She does not remember, that her mother's face beamed with joy only in some other moments. (Nāṣir, 50)

The feminine form أَيَّةٌ occurs only (but not always) before feminine or plural impersonal substantives.

اِكْتَشَفْتُ أَنَّنِي لَا أَمْلِكُ أَيَّةَ مَوْهِبَةٍ فِيهِ.

I have discovered that I have no skills [lit. skill] in it. (Šuqayr, 231)

أَمْ تَكُنْ هُنَاكَ أَيَّةُ شُرُوطٍ.

There were no conditions. (Al-Maḥādīn, 404)

لَمْ يُشِرْ إِلَى أَيِّ إِدَارَةٍ لِلْمَدْرَسَةِ.

He did not indicated any school administration. (Al-Maḥādīn, 67)

If genitive qualifier is to be definite, it is preceded by the preposition مِنْ :

كَانُوا غَيْرَ قَادِرِينَ عَلَى الْقِيَامِ بِمُعْظَمِ الْأَعْمَالِ السَّهْلَةِ فِى أَيٍّ مِنْ مَكَاتِبِ الْحُكُومَةِ.

They could not cope with most of simple activities at any of the government offices. (Al-Maḥādīn, 140)

- **Interrogative pronoun** أَيُّ – أَيَّةٌ ("what", "which", "what kind of")[24]

The phrases in which it occurs within interrogative sentences are similar to those in which it functions as indefinite pronoun.

---

[24]   Ibid., p. 698; R. Buckley, *Modern Literary Arabic...*, pp. 678–690.

أيَّ مُسْتَقْبَلٍ سَنَفْجَعُ بِهِ؟

What kind of future will we have to endure because of him? (Al-Kayyālī, 39)

أيَّ مَقْطَعٍ مِنْ أيِّ أُغْنِيَّةٍ غَنَّتْ؟

Which fragment of which song has she sung? (Nāṣir, 97)

أيُّ نَوْعٍ مِنَ الآبَاءِ هُوَ عَلِي؟

What kind of father [lit. of the fathers] is Ali? (Nāṣir, 58)

When as genitive qualifier there occurs a plural definite substantive,[25] the pronoun أيٌّ is a partitive:[26]

لا أدْرِي فِي أيِّ المَرَاحِلِ كَانَ عُضْوًا.

I do not know, which one of the stages he participated in. (Al-Maḥādīn, 41)

II. Definite substantive as a genitive qualifier

Phrases with a definite substantive[27] as a genitive qualifier are themselves definite, because (for instance):

- if they are followed by adjectival attributes, the attributes must be preceded by a definite article:

لِأحْلامِهِمْ الصَّغِيرَةِ المُتَمَرِّدَةِ وَغَرَائِزِهِمْ المَكْبُوتَةِ.

For their small, arrogant dreams and contained instincts. (Al-ʻAtīq, 63)

- if they are followed by indefinite adjectives, it results in nominal sentence.

فَضَاءُ المَدِينَةِ رَمَادِيٌّ.

The urban space is grey. (Šuqayr, 241)

---

25 R. Buckley, *Modern Literary Arabic...*, p. 678.

26 J. Danecki, *Gramatyka...*, p. 453.

27 A definite substantive it is a substantive with the definite article, with the genitival qualifier (definite substantive occurs as *nomen rectum*), with a (possessive) pronominal suffix or a proper name.

II. a) Definite singular substantive as a genitive qualifier

- **Substantive كُلّ ("totality", "whole", "all")**[28]

When followed by a definite singular substantive, it indicates entirety of 1-element set:

أَقْضِي كُلَّ الوَقْتِ فِي غُرْفَتِهِ الجَدِيدَةِ.

I spend all the time in his new room. (Al-'Atīq, 109)

هكذا تَمَّتْ تَغْطِيَةُ كُلِّ المِنْطَقَةِ المَرْكَزِيَّةِ.

In this way the whole central district got covered. (Al-Ahrām, 30.03.2011)

As *nomen rectum* there may occur a verbal noun. In the following example it occurs within the construction named cognate accusative[29] as the adverbial of manner ("fully", "completely", "thoroughly").

فَالطَّلَبَةُ يَقْتَدُونَ كُلَّ الإِقْتِدَاءِ بِأَعْمَالِ وَطَرِيقَةِ حَيَاةِ المُعَلِّمِ.

So, the students fully imitate [lit. imitate with full imitation] the deeds and the lifestyle of the teacher. (Al-Maḥādīn, 236)

As a genitive qualifier there may occur the pronoun هذا or ذٰلِكَ; the phrase means then "this all".

قَرَّرَ أَنْ يَهْرُبَ مِنْ كُلِّ هذا.

He decided to escape from this all. (Al-'Atīq, 38)

كُلُّ ذلِكَ يَقُودُ لِنَجَاحٍ بَاهِرٍ.

All this leads to amazing success. (Aš-Šarq al-Awsaṭ, 21.04.2011)

Phrases with the substantive كُلّ as *nomen regens* are semantically equivalent to the phrases with the same substantive (postpositive, standing in the agreement relation) as apposition, taking a (possessive) pronominal suffix referring to the determined substantive.

---

28 El-Said Badawi, M.G. Carter, A. Gully, *Modern Written Arabic...*, p. 224; R. Buckley, *Modern Literary Arabic...*, p. 183; J. Danecki, *Gramatyka...*, p. 53.

29 E. Górska, *Studium kontrastywne...*, pp. 305–310.

الْمَدِينَةُ كُلُّهَا هَادِئَةٌ.

The whole city is quiet. (Šuqayr, 210)

- **Substantive بَعْضٌ ("portion", "part", "some")**[30]

It is followed by uncountable (singular) substantives.

سَأَجِدُ بَعْضَ الرَّاحَةِ بَعِيدًا عَنْ تَنَاقُضَاتِ الوَضْعِ الإِنْتِقَالِيِّ.

I will find some comfort far from the adversities of changing fortunes. (Šuqayr, 235)

تَأْسِيسُ البَنْكِ الجَدِيدِ سَيَأْخُذُ بَعْضَ الوَقْتِ.

Establishing a new bank will take some time. (Aš-Šarq al-Awsaṭ, 5.05.2011)

- **Numeral أَوَّلُ ("first")**[31]

When followed by a definite singular substantive, it is a synonym of such substantives as بِدَايَةٌ and بَدْءٌ, and means "beginning".

سَيُفْتَحُ قِسْمٌ ثَانَوِيٌّ فِي أَوَّلِ العَامِ الدِّرَاسِيِّ القَادِمِ.

The secondary-school section will be opened at the beginning of the next school year. (Al-Maḥādīn, 312)

وَاسْتَمَرَّ القَلَقُ مِنْ أَوَّلِ الفَتْرَةِ الأُولَى.

The unrest has lasted since the beginning of the first period. (Al-Maḥādīn, 265)

- **Adjective آخِرُ ("last")**

When determined by a definite singular substantive, it function as a noun and means "end", "ending". It occurs as masculine regardless of the gender of *nomen rectum*.

إِلَى آخِرِ القَصِيدَةِ

To the end of the poem (Al-Kayyālī, 16)

---

[30] R. Buckley, *Modern Literary Arabic*..., p. 193; J. Danecki, *Gramatyka*..., p. 55.

[31] R. Buckley, *Modern Literary Arabic*..., p. 936.

عَدَدُ التِّلْمِيذَاتِ آخِرَ العَامِ كُنَّ 161.

Towards the end of the year the number of students amounted to 161. (Al-Maḥādīn, 425)

نَحْلُمُ أَنَّ مَرْكَبًا سَوْفَ يَجِيءُ مِنْ آخِرِ الدُّنْيَا.

We fantasize, that a ship will come from the end of the world. (Al-'Atīq, 44)

- **A substantive with more general meaning determined by a substantive with a more specific meaning or by a proper name of some object (so-called *genetivus epexegeticus*)**

The qualifier defines *nomen regens* naming it or giving its location, use, etc.[32]

مَدِينَةُ عَمَّانَ \ مَدِينَةُ حَلَبَ

City of Amman / City of Aleppo (Al-Kayyālī, 40)

إِلَى مَدِينَةِ (بُوبْرَاد)

To the city of Poprad (Al-Kayyālī, 150)

نَهْرُ دِجْلَة

Tigris river (Al-Kayyālī, 162)

يَوْمُ الجُمْعَةِ

(Day) Friday

شَهْرُ شُبَاطَ

(Month) February

[32] Ibid., pp. 171–172; C. Holes, *Modern Arabic...*, p. 205; E. Lipiński, *Semitic Languages...*, p. 499; K.C. Ryding, *A Reference Grammar of Modern Standard Arabic*, Cambridge University Press, Cambridge 2005, p. 206.

II. b) Definite plural substantive as a genitive qualifier

- **Substantives** كُلٌّ، كَافَّةً، جَمِيعٌ **("all")**[33]

They indicate the totality of some multi-element set. Substantive in the
function of *nomen rectum* is a centre of meaning of this phrase. It can be
easily seen in the way the agreement relation is being accomplished between those phrases and other components of sentences, and in the possibility of replacing them (except for كَافَّةً) with semantically equivalent
phrases with apposition.

لَمْ تَرَهُ فِي كُلِّ هَذِهِ السِّنِينَ.

She did not see him throughout all those years. (Nāṣir, 61)

أَجَبْتُ بِالنَّفْيِ عَنْ كُلِّ أَسْئِلَتِهَا.

I gave negative answers to all her questions. (Šuqayr, 27)

الصُّحُفُ كُلُّهَا تَقْرِيبًا تُشِيرُ إِلَى أَنَّ حَرْبًا قَدْ تَقَعُ.

All the newspapers point out, that a war will probably break out. (Šuqayr, 183)

تُنَمِّي رُوحَ الدَّيمُقْرَاطِيَّةِ فِي جَمِيعِ الْعَلَاقَاتِ الِاجْتِمَاعِيَّةِ.

It contributes to the rise of democratic spirit in all social relations. (Al-
Maḥādīn, 346)

وَقَدْ تَمَّ السَّمَاحُ لِجَمِيعِ الْمُوَظَّفِينَ غَيْرِ الْمُتَزَوِّجِينَ بِتَنَاوُلِ جَمِيعِ وَجَبَاتِهِمْ فِي بَيْتِ السَّكَنِ.

All unmarried employees were allowed to eat all their meals at home. (Al-
Maḥādīn, 213)

اللُّغَةُ الْعَرَبِيَّةُ هِيَ لُغَةُ التَّدْرِيسِ فِي جَمِيعِ الْمَدَارِسِ الْعَرَبِيَّةِ فِي كَافَّةِ أَجْزَاءِ الْوَطَنِ الْعَرَبِيِّ.

The Arabic language is a language of education in all Arab schools in all
parts of the Arab world. (Al-Maḥādīn, 354)

Substantives كُلٌّ، جَمِيعٌ used as apposition carry a (possessive) pronominal suffix referring to the determined substantive and agreeing with it
in number and gender.

---

[33]   El-Said Badawi, M.G. Carter, A. Gully, *Modern Written Arabic...*, pp. 224, 226–227,
230–231; R. Buckley, *Modern Literary Arabic...*, pp. 183, 189; J. Danecki, *Gramatyka...*, Vol. 2, pp. 53–54.

فَقَدْ بَقِيَتْ المَدَارِسُ جَمِيعُهَا مَفْتُوحَةً.

All the schools remained open. (Al-Maḥādīn, 180)

السِّيَاسِيُّونَ كُلُّهُمْ مُتَطَرِّفُونَ.

All the politicians are radical. (Aš-Šarq al-Awsaṭ, 14.01.2011)

- **Substantive بَعْضٌ ("some", "part", "portion")**[34]

If it is followed by countable substantives it is used similarly to كُلٌّ. It indicates a part of a multi-element set.

عِنْدَمَا فَتَحَتْ بَعْضُ المَدَارِسِ أَبْوَابَهَا.

When some of the schools got open. (Al-'Atīq, 60)

بَدَأَتْ تَتَحَقَّقُ فِيهِ بَعْضُ أَمَانِينَا.

Some of our wishes started to fullfil in it. (Al-Kayyālī, 107)

- **Substantive مُعْظَمٌ ("most", "majority")**[35]

It indicates a substantial part of a multi-element set. It is used similarly to بَعْضٌ.

مُعْظَمُ أَفْرَادِ الأُسْرَةِ الحَاكِمَةِ يَعِيشُونَ فِيهَا.

Most members of the royal family live in it. (Al-Maḥādīn, 59)

كَانَ مُعْظَمُ بَنَاتِ وَأَوْلَادِ الحَيِّ يُرَدِّدُونَ الاِبْتِهَالَاتِ فِي شَهْرِ رَمَضَانَ.

The majority of girls and boys from the district repeated prayers during Ramadan. (Al-Kayyālī, 86)

---

[34] El-Said Badawi, M.G. Carter, A. Gully, *Modern Written Arabic...*, p. 193; R. Buckley, *Modern Literary Arabic...*, p. 193; J. Danecki, *Gramatyka...*, p. 55.

[35] El-Said Badawi, M.G. Carter, A. Gully, *Modern Written Arabic...*, p. 229; R. Buckley, *Modern Literary Arabic...*, p. 200.

- **Substantive عَدَدٌ ("number")**[36]

It is used similarly to substantive بَعْضٌ (also with countable substantives).

عَرَفْتُ أَنَّ عَدَدَ سُكَّانِهَا مِلْيُونَانِ مِنَ البَشَرِ.

I knew, that the number of inhabitants amounts to 2 millions. (Šuqayr, 214)

If it is followed by an adjectival attribute, a genitival qualifier is replaced by a prepositional phrase with the preposition مِنْ, having partitive meaning:

تُحِيطُ بِهِ عَدَدٌ كَبِيرٌ مِنَ النِّسَاءِ.

A huge number of women surrounds him. (Al-Kayyālī, 17)

كَانَ عَدَدٌ قَلِيلٌ مِنَ النَّاسِ قَدْ وَصَلُوا إِلَى المَكَانِ.

A small number of people has arrived there. (Šuqayr, 89)

Prepositional phrase may also be used, when the substantive عَدَدٌ is not followed by an adjectival attribute, and then it indicates some indefinite number of objects.

تَنَاوَلْتُ طَعَامَ العَشَاءِ مَعَ عَدَدٍ مِنَ النِّسَاءِ وَالرِّجَالِ.

I had a dinner with some women and men (lit. "some of the women and men"). (Šuqayr, 212)

- **Numerals meaning tens, hundreds, thousands, millions, etc.**[37]

These numerals may be used similarly to plural substantives. In such phrases as *nomen rectum* appear definite plural substantives in the genitive case.

شُوهِدَ عَشَرَاتُ المُتَظَاهِرِينَ المُضَرَّجِينَ بِالدِّمَاءِ يَتَلَقَّوْنَ العِلاَجَ.

There have been seen dozens of demonstrators stained with blood, who were subject to medical treatment. (Aš-Šarq al-Awsaṭ, 19.03.2011)

مُنْذُ آلاَفِ السِّنِينَ

For thousands years (Al-Kayyālī, 140)

---

36 R. Buckley, *Modern Literary Arabic...*, p. 932.

37 Ibid., pp. 930–931.

أشِيرُ إلَى أنَّ مِئَاتِ الصَّفَحَاتِ هذِهِ كَتَبْتُهَا بِخَطِّ يَدِي.

I [would like to] point out, that these hundreds of pages I have written by hand. (Al-Maḥādīn, 8)

- **Numeral أَحَدٌ ("one of" – masculine)**[38]

It indicates one element of a multi-element set containing objects named with masculine substantives.

سَمِعْنَا أَحَدَ الرِّجَالِ.

We heared one of the men. (Al-Kayyālī, 36)

وَصَلَتْنَا دَعْوَةٌ مِنْ أَحَدِ الأَقَارِبِ.

There arrived an invitation from one of the relatives. (Al-Kayyālī, 40)

- **Numeral إِحْدَى ("one of" – feminine)**

It indicates one element of a multi-element set containing objects named with feminine substantives.

فَتَحَتْ لِي إِحْدَى المُجَنَّدَاتِ البَابَ.

One of the female recruits opened the door for me. (Al-Kayyālī, 135)

إِحْدَى سَيِّدَاتِ المُخَيَّمِ

One of the ladies [from] the camp. (Al-Kayyālī, 77)

- **Ordinal numeral أَوَّلُ ("first")**[39]

It indicates the first element chosen from a set of objects named with countable substantives.

كَانَتْ هذِهِ أَوَّلَ الخُطُوَاتِ العَمَلِيَّةِ لإِلْحَاقِ التَّعْلِيمِ.

These were the first practical attempts to start teaching. (Al-Maḥādīn, 143)

---

38 El-Said Badawi, M.G. Carter, A. Gully, *Modern Written Arabic*..., p. 258; R. Buckley, *Modern Literary Arabic*..., p. 912.

39 El-Said Badawi, M.G. Carter, A. Gully, *Modern Written Arabic*..., p. 271.

فِي أوَّلِ أيَّامِ العَيْدِ

On the first day (lit. "the first of the days") of the holiday. (Al-Kayyālī, 113)

كَانَتْ أوَّلَ قَصَائِدِي.

It was the first of my poems. (Al-Kayyālī, 80)

This numeral can occur as feminine (أُولَى). It is then an equivalent of a phrase consisting of a feminine substantive and an ordinal numeral in function of adjectival attribute.

أوْضَحَ أنَّ حَضَارَةَ مِصْرَ هي أُولَى الحَضَارَاتِ فِي التَّارِيخِ القَدِيمِ.

He explained, that the Egiptian civilisation is the first one of the ancient civilisations. (Aš-Šarq al-Awsaṭ, 12.04.2011)

الحَاجَةُ إلَى الدِّينِ هِيَ أُولَى الحَاجَاتِ النَّفْسِيَّةِ لِلإِنْسَانِ.

Need for a religion is the first of human needs. (Al-Maḥādīn, 352)

خِلاَلَ يَوْمِ الجُمْعَةِ المَاضِي خَرَجَتْ أُولَى المُظَاهَرَاتِ فِي حَيِّ المَيْدَانِ فِي دِمَشْقَ.

Last Friday the first demonstration took [to the streets] in the area of the Square in Damascus. (Al-Ahrām, 10.05.2011)

- **Other ordinal numerals (2–10)**[40]

They are used similarly to the numeral أوَّل. They indicate successive elements of a set.

أرْجَأتْ مَحْكَمَةُ جِنَايَاتِ السُّوَيْسِ ثَانِي جِلْسَاتِهَا.

The Swedish criminal court delayed the second of its sessions. (Aš-Šarq al-Awsaṭ, 9.05.2011)

عَنْ تَارِيخِ خَامِسِ مُلُوكِ الدَّوْلَةِ السَّعُودِيَّةِ

On the history of the fifth king of the Saudi state (Aš-Šarq al-Awsaṭ, 5.04.2011)

- **Ordinal numeral أوَائِل ("first" – plural)**[41]

It occurs in plural and means "beginning", "first days", "early".

---

40 Ibid., p. 272.

41 R. Buckley, *Modern Literary Arabic…*, pp. 936–937.

إِلَى أَوَائِلِ السِّتِّينَاتِ

Till the beginning of the sixties. (Al-Maḥādīn, 556)

- **Adjective آخِرٌ („last" – singular)**

It indicates the last element chosen from a set of objects named with countable substantives.

حِينَ كَانَ شَارِعُهُمْ يُوَدِّعُ آخِرَ أَنْفَاسِ شَمْسِ الغُرُوبِ.

When their street saw off the last of the gleams of the setting sun. (Al-'Atīq, 29)

حِينَ تُسْتَرْجَعُ آخِرُ كَلِمَاتِهِ فِي هذَا الحِوَارِ.

When his last word from that conversation is being quoted. (Nāṣir, 82)

- **Adjective أَوَاخِرُ („last" – plural)**

In plural it means "end" and precedes substantives naming time units (month, year, decade, century).

هَاجَرُوا إِلَيْهَا أَوَاخِرَ القَرْنِ التَّاسِعَ عَشَرَ.

They emigrated there towards the end of the nineteenth century. (Šuqayr, 112)

اسْتَمَرَّتْ فَتْرَةُ الدِّرَاسَةِ حَتَّى أَوَاخِرِ الثَّلاَثِينَاتِ.

The period of education lasted till the end of the thirties. (Al-Maḥādīn, 417)

تَعْلِيمُ المَرْأَةِ بَدَأَ فِى أَوَاخِرِ العَقْدِ الثَّالِثِ مِنَ القَرْنِ العِشْرِينَ.

Women's education started towards the end of the third decade of the twentieth century. (Al-Maḥādīn, 404)

- **Adjective مُخْتَلِفٌ ("various", "different")**

If it occurs as *nomen regens*, it is in masculine gender and functions as a noun meaning "diversity".[42]

ثَمَّةَ سَيَّارَاتٌ مِنْ مُخْتَلِفِ الأَشْكَالِ وَالأَلْوَانِ.

There are cars of various shapes and colours. (Šuqayr, 11)

---

42 Ibid., pp. 175–176.

نَامَ فِيهَا مُلُوكٌ وَأَمِيرَاتٌ وَنُجُومُ سِينَمَا مِنْ مُخْتَلِفِ الجِنْسِيَّاتِ.

There slept in it kings, princesses and movie stars of various nationalities. (Aš-Šarq al-Awsaṭ, 28.04.2011)

This component of the phrase is formally a determined one. The whole phrase is equivalent to a phrase consisting of a substantive determined by an adjectival attribute – adjective مُخْتَلِفٌ follows a substantive and stays in agreement relation to it.

تَحَدَّثْنَا عَنِ الدِّيَانَاتِ المُخْتَلِفَةِ.

We have been talking about different religions. (Šuqayr, 95)

يُعَبِّرُ عَنْهَا المُفَكِّرُونَ المُخْتَلِفُونَ.

They are expressed by various intelectuals. (Al-Ahrām, 02.09.2010)

- **Masculine elative adjective (أَفْعَلُ)**[43]

It is used (in the masculine gender) for a superlative when followed by plural masculine and feminine substantives.

فِيهَا أَجْمَلُ الأَحْيَاءِ.

There are the most beautiful of the districts there. (Šuqayr, 190)

(The substantive حَيٌّ is masculine).

الرَّئِيسُ السَّادَاتُ مِنْ أَلْطَفِ الشَّخْصِيَّاتِ الَّتِي لَقِيتُهَا.

President as-Sadat is one of the most likeable personage I have ever met. (Aš-Šarq al-Awsaṭ, 7.11.2010)

(Substantive شَخْصِيَّةٌ is feminine).

The context enables us to decide, whether an elative refers to the only one element which has some feature to the highest degree, or to some of them.

هُوَ أَصْغَرُ الأَبْنَاءِ.

He is the youngest of the sons. (Al-Kayyālī, 113)

---

43 El-Said Badawi, M.G. Carter, A. Gully, *Modern Written Arabic...*, pp. 251–252; R. Buckley, *Modern Literary Arabic...*, p. 636.

قَالَ إِنَّ رِجَالَ الدِّينِ هُمْ أَكْثَرُ النَّاسِ قُدْرَةً عَلَى نَشْرِ السَّمَاحَةِ وَالسَّلَامِ.

He said that theologians have the highest capabilities [lit. are of the highest capability] as to promote tolerance and peace. (Al-Ahrām, 6.05.2011)

- **Feminine elative adjective (فُعْلَى)[44]**

Additionally it is used for a superlative when followed by feminine impersonal substantives.

طِوَالَ فَتْرَةِ إِقَامَتِهِ فِي كُبْرَى الْمُدُنِ الْأَسْتُرَالِيَّةِ (مَدِينَةِ مَلْبُورْن)

During his stay in the largest of Australian cities (Melbourne) (Aš-Šarq al-Awsaṭ, 12.04.2011)

كَانَ قَدْ دَرَسَ فِي جَامِعَةِ مَدْرِيدَ الكومبلوتنسية، كُبْرَى جَامِعَاتِ الْعَاصِمَةِ الْإِسْبَانِيَّةِ.

He studied at the Universidad Complutense de Madrid, the largest of the universities of the capital of Spain. (Aš-Šarq al-Awsaṭ, 10.04.2011)

- **Plural feminine elative adjective كُبْرَيَاتٌ ("largest", "biggest")**

As plural feminine elative with the suffix -ātun it is followed by feminine impersonal substantives.[45]

عَادَ الْهُدُوءُ لِمَدِينَةِ الزَّاوِيَةِ (رَابِعَةِ كُبْرَيَاتِ الْمُدُنِ فِي الْغَرْبِ اللِّيبِيِّ).

The peace has returned to the city of Az-Zāwiya (the fourth largest city of [the cities of] western Libya). (Aš-Šarq al-Awsaṭ, 27.02.2011)

أَصْبَحَتْ الْآنَ مِنْ كُبْرَيَاتِ الْجَمْعِيَّاتِ الْخَيْرِيَّةِ.

It became one of the biggest [of the] charity organizations. (Aš-Šarq al-Awsaṭ, 24.01.2011)

شَهِدَ وَاحِدَةً مِنْ كُبْرَيَاتِ مُظَاهَرَاتِهِ.

He witnessed one of the biggest of the manifestations. (Aš-Šarq al-Awsaṭ, 2.02.2011)

---

[44] El-Said Badawi, M.G. Carter, A. Gully, *Modern Written Arabic…*, p. 252.
[45] Ibid.

- **Adjective كِبَارٌ („great" – plural)**

It is followed by plural personal substantives and means "great", "eminent".

يُعْتَبَرُ أَحَدَ كِبَارِ المُهْتَمِّينَ بِتَارِيخِ العَرَبِ فِي الأَنْدَلُسِ.

He is counted among eminent experts of the history of the Arabs in Andalusia. (Aš-Šarq al-Awsaṭ, 12.04.2011)

أَصْبَحَ الآنَ مِنْ كِبَارِ رِجَالِ الأَعْمَالِ.

He became one of great businessmen. (Nāṣir, 48)

- **Adjective قُدَمَاءُ ("ancient" – plural)**

It is followed by plural personal substantives and means "ancient".

كَانَ يَرْمُزُ عِنْدَ قُدَمَاءِ المِصْرِيِّينَ إِلَي بَعْثِ الحَيَاةِ.

For ancient Egyptians it symbolized revival of life. (Al-Ahrām, 25.04.2011)

تَحْكِي قِصَصَ قُدَمَاءِ الصِّينِيِّينَ.

It tells the stories of ancient Chinese. (Aš-Šarq al-Awsaṭ, 25.09.2010)

This adjective occurs also as an adjectival attribute following plural personal substantives and staing in the agreement relation to them.

اِهْتَمَّ المِصْرِيُّونَ القُدَمَاءُ كَثِيرًا فِي حَيَاتِهِمْ.

Ancient Egyptians were very much interested in their lives. (Aš-Šarq al-Awsaṭ, 4.11.2010)

II. c) Definite dual substantive as a genitive qualifier

- **Substantive كِلا ("both" – masculine, feminine)**

It is determined by a masculine or feminine substantive. In this case it is an uninflected word.[46]

46 R. Buckley, *Modern Literary Arabic...*, p. 198; J. Danecki, *Gramatyka...*, pp. 55–56.

تَتَمَثَّلُ فِي تَلاَشِي ثِقَةِ الأَعْضَاءِ فِي كِلاَ الحِزْبَيْنِ.

They manifest in decreasing trust of the members of both parties. (Aš-Šarq al-Awsaṭ, 7.05.2011)

أُسِّسَتْ فُصُولٌ مِنْ كِلاَ المَدْرَسَتَيْنِ.

The departments were formed out of both schools. (Al-Maḥādīn, 481)

When determined by a possessive pronoun, the substantive كِلاَ inflects as dual substantives in the construct state (*status constructus*).

كِلاَهُمَا دَخَلاَ بِتَأْشِيرَةِ سِيَاحَةٍ.

They both entered with tourist visa. (Aš-Šarq al-Awsaṭ, 8.05.2011)

أَكَّدَ أَنَّ كِلَيْهِمَا جَاءَا لِيُبَرْهِنَ عَنْ بَرَاءَتِهِمَا.

He assured that they both came so that he would prove their innocence. (Aš-Šarq al-Awsaṭ, 12.02.2011)

This substantive may also occur as uninflected one with a (possessive) pronominal suffix.

فَقَدُوا أَحَدَ العَيْنَيْنِ أَوْ كِلاَهُمَا.

Each of them lost one eye or both of them. (Al-Ahrām, 9.05.2011)

اِفْتَرَضُوا التَّنْظِيمَ الجَيِّدَ لِلْمُرُورِ سَوَاءً عَنْ طَرِيقِ الشُّرْطَةِ أَوِ المُتَطَوِّعِينَ أَوْ كِلاَهُمَا مَعاً.

They introduced a satisfactory traffic organization with the help of the police, of volunteers, or of both of them simultaneously. (Al-Ahrām, 19.05.2011)

When a phrase with the substantive كِلاَ is a sentence subject, then the verb, which is a predicate of a sentence (when following the subject), is in dual (as above). If the predicate is in singular, the phrase means „each one of the two of them". The same is the case, when the phrase is replaced by an anaphoric pronoun referring to it.

عَرَفُوا أَنَّ كِلَيْهِمَا وُلِدَ لأَبٍ مَجْنُونٍ.

They have learned, that each of [the two of] them had been born to an insane father. (Aš-Šarq al-Awsaṭ, 10.05.2011)

كِلاَهُمَا يَعْمَلُ فِي حَقْلِ الإِبْدَاعِ عَلَى نَحْوٍ مُشَابِهٍ.

Each of [the two of] them does the artistic work in a similar way. (Aš-Šarq al-Awsaṭ, 18.05.2011)

مِصْرُ وَتُرْكِيَا أَيْضاً كِلاَهُمَا عِنْدَهُ رَصِيدُ إِبْدَاعٍ ثَقَافِيٌّ وَافِرٌ.

Each of Egypt and Turkey has considerable cultural achievements. (Al-Ahrām, 10.03.2011)

- **Substantive كِلْتَا ("both" – feminine)**

It is a variant of كِلَا that may replace it in phrases with a feminine substantive as qualifier. It is uninflected when followed by a substantive, and inflected for case when it takes a (possessive) pronominal suffix.

هذِهِ الزِّيَارَةُ فُرْصَةٌ مُمْتَازَةٌ لِتَحْفِيزِ رِجَالِ الأَعْمَالِ فِي كِلْتَا الدَّوْلَتَيْنِ.

This visit is an excellent opportunity to stimulate businessmen in both countries. (Aš-Šarq al-Awsaṭ, 28.04.2011)

يَسْتَخْدِمُهَا المُتَطَرِّفُونَ فِي كِلْتَا الدِّيَانَتَيْنِ.

The extremists of both religions use them. (Al-Ahrām, 16.01.2011)

لأَنَّ صِرْبِيَا وَكُوسُوفُو كِلْتَيْهِمَا تَمْلِكَانِ الوَثَائِقَ.

Because both Serbia and Kosovo are in possession of those documents. (Aš-Šarq al-Awsaṭ, 16.07.2010)

II. d) Definite singular, dual or plural substantive as a genitive qualifier

- **Substantive نَفْسٌ ("same")**

In genitive constructions this substantive occurs as singular, and is followed by singular, dual or plural definite substantives as its qualifiers.[47]

تَحَدَّثْنَا فِي نَفْسِ المَوْضُوعِ.

We talked about the same subject. (Al-Kayyālī, 150)

عُيِّنَ فِي نَفْسِ مَدَارِسِ المُخَيَّمِ.

He got nominated at the same schools of the camp. (Al-Kayyālī, 87)

---

[47] R. Buckley, *Modern Literary Arabic…*, pp. 253–254; J. Danecki, *Gramatyka…*, p. 54; K.C. Ryding, *A Reference Grammar…*, pp. 219–220.

لاَ يُمْكِنُ أَنْ يَكُونُوا نَفْسَ الأَشْخَاصِ الآنَ.

They cannot be the same persons now. (Al-Ahrām, 15.03.2011)

Phrases with the substantive نَفْسٌ as *nomen regens* are semantically equivalent to the phrases with the same substantive (postpositive, standing in the agreement relation) as apposition, taking a (possessive) pronominal suffix referring to the determined substantive. When the head of a phrase is plural, then the substantive نَفْسٌ occurs also in plural (أَنْفُسٌ) and takes a plural pronominal suffix.[48]

كَانَا يَلْعَبَانِ الدَّوْرَ الثَّقَافِيَّ نَفْسَهُ.

They were playing the same role in culture. (Al-Maḥādīn, 106)

الَّتِي تَنْشَبُ بَيْنَ القَرَوِيِّينَ أَنْفُسِهِمْ.

Which are breaking out between the same peasants. (Šuqayr, 164)

- **Substantive مِثْلٌ ("like", "such a")[49]**

تَكْثُرُ حَوَادِثُ الاِنْتِحَارِ بَيْنَ أَهْلِ البِلاَدِ فِي مِثْلِ هَذَا الطَّقْسِ!

In such weather suicides are numerous among the population of the country. (Šuqayr, 243)

لَمْ أَرَ دِجْلَةَ فِي مِثْلِ هذا الجَمَالِ.

I have never seen Tigris river so beautiful. [lit. of such beauty]. (Al-Kayyālī, 162)

لاَ تُرِيدُ أَنْ تُصْبِحَ إِحْدَى الفَتَاتَيْنِ مِثْلَهَا.

She does not want to become one of the girls such as her [referring to some other person]. (Nāṣir, 38)

مَعَ نَدْرَةِ مِثْلِ هؤُلاَءِ المُسْتَغْنِيِّينَ العُظَمَاءِ فِي مُجْتَمَعِنَا الحَالِيِّ.

In spite of the rarity of very rich men in our society today. (Al-Ahrām, 22.01.2011)

---

48 El-Said Badawi, M.G. Carter, A. Gully, *Modern Written Arabic*..., p. 224; J. Danecki, *Gramatyka*..., p. 54.

49 El-Said Badawi, M.G. Carter, A. Gully, *Modern Written Arabic*..., p. 232; R. Buckley, *Modern Literary Arabic*..., p. 202; J. Danecki, *Gramatyka*..., p. 56.

III. Indefinite or definite substantive as genitive qualifier

This group contains phrases, in which definiteness or indefiniteness of the qualifier does not affect the meaning of the whole phrase and results only in its definiteness or indefiniteness (in Arabic they constitute substantial majority of genitive constructions). The choice between them is dictated by syntactic rules. I mention them only for the sake of comparison with the phrases analyzed above. I give examples of constructions including as *nomen regens* substantives, that due to their productivity in word formation appear frequently in Arabic texts.

- **Substantive عَدَمٌ ("lack")**

It is used mainly as negation of verbal nouns.[50]

أَظُنُّ أَنَّهُ كَانَ فِي حَالَةِ عَدَمِ التَّحَمُّلِ لِمَا حَصَلَ لَنَا.

I think, that he lacked toleration for what had happened to us. (Al-Kayyālī, 71)

بِحُجَّةِ عَدَمِ وُجُودِ أَمَاكِنَ شَاغِرَةٍ لَدَيْهِ.

On the pretext that there is no free places [lit. lack of free places]. (Šuqayr, 128)

كَانَتْ هُنَاكَ مُشْكِلَةٌ أُخْرَى وَهِيَ عَدَمُ وُجُودِ سَاعَةِ حَائِطٍ.

There was another problem there – it was a lack of a wall clock. (Al-Maḥādīn, 522)

- **Substantive غَيْرٌ ("not", "other", "not this")**

It negates meaning of the word determining it. It occurs in phrases with substantives or adjectives as *nomen rectum*.[51]

فِي النَّهَارِ زَارَتْنَا إِحْدَى الجَارَاتِ عَلَى غَيْرِ مَوْعِدٍ.

During the day one of our neighbours visited us unexpectedly [not at the agreed time]. (Al-Kayyālī, 59)

---

[50] El-Said Badawi, M.G. Carter, A. Gully, *Modern Written Arabic...*, p. 326; R. Buckley, *Modern Literary Arabic...*, p. 730; J. Danecki, *Gramatyka...*, p. 55; K.C. Ryding, *A Reference Grammar...*, pp. 218–219.

[51] El-Said Badawi, M.G. Carter, A. Gully, *Modern Written Arabic...*, pp. 233–236; J. Danecki, *Gramatyka...*, p. 55; K.C. Ryding, *A Reference Grammar...*, p. 223.

خَرَجْتُ مِنَ الفُنْدُقِ عَلَى غَيْرِ هُدًى.

I left the hotel with no specific aim. (Al-Kayyālī, 146)

هِيَ غَيْرُ مُتَزَوِّجَةٍ.

She is not married. (Šuqayr, 119)

لَكِنَّ هُنَاكَ عَدَداً غَيْرَ قَلِيلٍ مِنَ الأَطْفَالِ فِي سِنِّ المَدْرَسَةِ.

There is quite a lot [not a small number of] school-age children. (Al-Maḥādīn, 328)

إِنَّ كُلَّ امْرَأَةٍ غَيْرِ مُحَجَّبَةٍ مَسْؤُولَةٌ عَمَّا قَدْ يَقَعُ عَلَيْهَا.

Every woman with no veil [not veiled] is responsible for what may happen to her. (Nāṣir, 43)

- **Substantive ذُو ("owner", "possessor")**

This word occurs in various genders and numbers and inflects for case. It designates a person or thing having attribute indicated by *nomen rectum*.[52]

Singular, masculine (in nominative, genitive and accusative): ذُو، ذِي، ذَا
Singular, feminine: ذَاتُ، ذَاتِ، ذَاتَ
Dual, masculine: ذَوَا، ذَوَيْ، ذَوَيْ
Dual, feminine: ذَوَتَا، ذَوَتَيْ، ذَوَتَيْ
Plural, masculine personal: ذَوُو، ذَوِي، ذَوِي
Plural, feminine personal: ذَوَاتُ، ذَوَاتِ، ذَوَاتِ.

ثَمَّةَ نَادِلٌ آخَرُ، عِرَاقِيٌّ ذُو وَجْهٍ أَسْمَرَ.

There is other waiter, a dark-faced Iraqi. (Šuqayr, 130)

ثُمَّ أَوْصَلَنِي مُحَمَّدٌ إِلَى فُنْدُقِ زَيْنَبَ ذِي الطَّوَابِقِ الخَمْسَةِ.

Then Muḥammad brought me to the five-storey hotel Zaynab. (Šuqayr, 257)

تَمَّ إِعَارَةُ 12 مُدَرِّساً مِصْرِيّاً مِنْ ذَوِي الخِبْرَةِ العَالَمِيَّةِ.

Twelwe Egyptian teachers with a worldwide experience have been hired. (Al-Maḥādīn, 229)

52 El-Said Badawi, M.G. Carter, A. Gully, *Modern Written Arabic*..., pp. 139–142; R. Buckley, *Modern Literary Arabic*..., pp. 179–182; J. Danecki, *Gramatyka*..., pp. 56–57.

ذَكَرْتُ أَسْمَاءَ اثْنَيْنِ مِنْ رِجَالِ الدِّينِ ذَوِي الشَّخْصِيَّاتِ التَّرْبَوِيَّةِ.

I mentioned names of two theologians with pedagogical personalities. (Al-Maḥādīn, 150)

كَانَتْ اللَّجْنَةُ التَّنْفِيذِيَّةُ العُلْيَا ذَاتَ نُفُوذٍ كَبِيرٍ.

The Supreme Executive Council was very powerful. (Al-Maḥādīn, 301)

عَدَدُ النِّسَاءِ اللَّائِي سَيَحْضُرْنَ المُنْتَدَى مِنَ السَّيِّدَاتِ ذَوَاتِ النُّفُوذِ المَالِيِّ وَالتِّجَارِيِّ.

Number of women, who will visit the forum, from among ladies influential in finance and trade. (Aš-Šarq al-Awsaṭ, 26.01.2011)

- **Substantive صَاحِبٌ ("owner", "possessor")**

Its meaning is similar to ذُو. It occurs in both masculine (صَاحِبٌ) and feminine (صَاحِبَةٌ) genders.[53]

الحُرِّيَّةُ تَعْنِي أَنَّهُ مِنْ حَقِّ كُلِّ صَاحِبِ رَأْيٍ التَّعْبِيرُ عَنْ رَأْيِهِ.

Freedom means that everybody, who holds any view [lit. holder of the view], has right to express it. (Aš-Šarq al-Awsaṭ, 14.05.2011)

إِنَّ مِصْرَ لَمْ تَعُدْ صَاحِبَةَ مَوْقِفٍ يَرْفُضُ التَّعَامُلَ مَعَ حَرَكَةِ حَمَاسٍ.

The approach of Egypt does not assumes refusal to cooperate with the Hamas movement any more. (Aš-Šarq al-Awsaṭ, 2.05.2011)

صَاحِبُ البَقَّالَةِ إِيرَانِيٌّ.

The owner of the grocery is an Iranian. (Šuqayr, 243)

This substantive is also used in titles, names of offices.[54]

صَاحِبُ العَظَمَةِ \ صَاحِبُ السُمُوِّ

His Majesty / His Highness (Al-Maḥādīn, 236)

---

53 R. Buckley, *Modern Literary Arabic…*, p. 178.

54 El-Said Badawi, M.G. Carter, A. Gully, *Modern Written Arabic…*, pp. 142–143; K.C. Ryding, *A Reference Grammar…*, p. 219.

- **Substantive رَجُلٌ ("man")**

It is used in phrases designating persons, who operate – often professionally – in the field indicated by a genitive qualifier, e.g. رَجُلُ أَعْمَالٍ (businessman), رَجُلُ سِيَاسَةٍ (political activist).[55]

In plural – رِجَالٌ – this substantive designate professional groups or groups of people acting together, e.g. رِجَالُ السِّلْكِ الدِّبْلُومَاسِيِّ (diplomats), رِجَالُ التَّعْلِيمِ (pedagogues), رِجَالُ اللاَّهُوتِ (clergy),[56] رِجَالُ إِطْفَاءٍ (firemen, fire brigade).

- **Substantive سَيِّدَةٌ ("woman", "lady")**

It is (in numerous cases) a feminine counterpart of the word رَجُلٌ.

قَالَتْ إِنَّهَا سَيِّدَةُ أَعْمَالٍ.

She said that she was a businesswoman. (Aš-Šarq al-Awsaṭ, 30.05.2011)

حَضَرَ الاِحْتِفَالَ لَفِيفٌ مِنْ سَيِّدَاتِ السِّيَاسَةِ وَالمُجْتَمَعِ الفَرَنْسِيَّاتِ وَالعَرَبِيَّاتِ.

In the celebration there participated a group of the French and Arab political and social female activists. (Aš-Šarq al-Awsaṭ, 13.04.2011)

رَأَتْ إِحْدَى سَيِّدَاتِ القَرْيَةِ.

She saw one of the peasant women. (Al-Ahrām, 25.12.2010)

كَانَتْ كَيْكُو بِمَثَابَةِ سَيِّدَةِ بِيرُو الأُولَى.

Keiko was an equivalent of the first lady of Peru. (Aš-Šarq al-Awsaṭ, 20.03.2011)

- **Substantive أَهْلٌ ("family", "population", "inhabitants")[57]**

It occurs in phrases designating groups of people that live or work or go in for some other activities together, e.g. أَهْلُ الأَدَبِ وَالفَنِّ (writers and artists), أَهْلُ الجَنَّةِ (those who are in Paradise), أَهْلُ العِلْمِ (scholars).[58]

يَتَمَشَّى فِيهِ أُنَاسٌ مِنْ أَهْلِ المَدِينَةِ.

There stroll on it some of the inhabitants of the city. (Šuqayr, 13)

---

55 J. Danecki, J. Kozłowska, *Słownik arabsko-polski*, Wiedza Powszechna, Warszawa 1996, p. 369.

56 H.K. Baranov, *Bolshoy arabsko-russkiy slovar*, Moscow 2008, pp. 289, 475.

57 R. Buckley, *Modern Literary Arabic...*, p. 177.

58 H.K. Baranov, *Bolshoy arabsko-russkiy...*, pp. 48–49.

Conclusion

In Modern Standard Arabic the genitive constructions as *nomen regens* contain substantives as well as adjectives and numerals (following syntactic rules of a substantive). As *nomen rectum* there occur substantives. The grammatical properties of the latter are determined by the meaning of the whole phrase or by the syntactic demands within the sentence.

The indefinite substantive as genitival qualifier occurs obligatory (as determined by the meaning of the phrase) only in few cases:

(a) in singular – when as *nomen regens* there occur (i) elative adjectives, ordinal numerals, the adjective آخِر, the substantive كُلّ (meaning "every", "each"), which indicate a „place" of the object in the set of similar objects, and (ii) cardinal numerals meaning hundreds, thousands, millions etc.;

(b) in plural – when as *nomen regens* there occur cardinal numerals 3–10, the quantifier بِضْعَة (meaning „some", „a few", „several") and the substantive عِدَّة (meaning „a number") which all define some set quantitatively;

(c) in singular or plural when as *nomen regens* there occur the pronoun أَيّ (as indefinite pronoun or interrogative pronoun) or the participle مُجَرَّد.

In such phrases (a–c) it is *nomen rectum* (genitival qualifier) that is a centre of meaning. All genitive constructions with indefinite qualifiers are themselves indefinite. If definite expressions are needed, genitive constructions are being replaced with phrases with appositions or with adjectival attributes. In such phrases, *nomen rectum* of genitive construction becomes a determined component, and *nomen regens* – a determining component standing to the head of the phrase in the agreement relation.

As a genitival qualifier there may occur a substantive – obligatory a definite one.[59] It denotes a set (1-element or multi-element), while the determined component designates an element (or elements) occupying some particular position within the set, being its part or whole, or having a specific feature. Such constructions are frequent in Modern Standard Arabic, and are used to isolate subsets within sets. The examples presented above indicate, that similarity of forms results in similarity of meanings. They have mainly a partitive meaning (*genetivus partitivus*,

59 A definite substantive it is a substantive with the definite article, with the genitival qualifier (definite substantive occurs as *nomen rectum*), with a (possessive) pronominal suffix or a proper name.

the partitive genitive[60]). In phrases which demand definite genitive qualifiers, in the function of the latter there occur only substantives. They refer to a set (1-element or multi-element), and the referent of a head of the phrase occupies is its subset, as:

- the whole set (كُلّ، كَافَّة، جَمِيع، كِلاَ، كِلْتَا),
- part of the set (بَعْض),
- majority (مُعْظَم),
- specific number (عَدَد),
- part consisting of tens, hundreds, thousands, millions etc. of elements (عَشَرَات، مِئَات، آلاف، أُلوف، مَلاَيِين),
- element or elements having some feature to the highest degree (*superlativus*),
- element or elements being first (أَوَّل، أُولَى), subsequent (ثَانٍ، ثَالِث...) or last (آخِر) element(s),
- element being the beginning (أَوَّل، أَوَائِل) or end (آخِر، أَوَاخِر) of a set,
- element being one of the elements of the set (أَحَدٌ، إِحْدَى).

In the phrases of this kind there also occur expressions designating the same object (نَفْس) or similar object (مِثْل) or having a limiting meaning (*genetivus epexegeticus*).

As heads of phrases there occur substantives and substantivized ordinal numerals or adjectives. This kind of usage of adjectives and numerals is quite frequent in Modern Standard Arabic.[61]

The most of the Arabic substantives may be used in the function of genitival qualifier as both indefinite and definite. It depends of syntactic function of the whole phrase, which may demand its indefiniteness or definiteness. In this group there are for instance substantives very productive in word formation, such as أَهْلٌ , سَيِّدَةٌ , رَجُلٌ , صَاحِبٌ , ذُو (personal substantives being components of expressions (juxtapositions) designating people having some common feature, of the same profession or social group (class), as well as substantives غَيْرٌ , عَدَمٌ used to negate a substantive or adjective.

In all the groups of genitival phrases discussed in this paper, their determined components precede determiners, and irrespective of which part of speech they represent, they follow syntactic rules of a substantive.

---

60 K. Polański (ed.), *Encyklopedia językoznawstwa…*, p. 172; E. Lipiński, *Semitic Languages…*, p. 498; V. Cantarino, *Syntax of Modern Arabic…* p. 112; K.C. Ryding, *A Reference Grammar…*, pp. 206–207.

61 E. Lipiński, *Semitic Languages…*, p. 499.

References

Badawi El-Said, Carter M.G., Gully A., *Modern Written Arabic: A Comprehensive Grammar*, Routledge, London–New York 2004.

Buckley R., *Modern Literary Arabic. A Reference Grammar*, Librairie du Liban Publ., Beirut 2004.

Cantarino V., *Syntax of Modern Arabic Prose. The Expanded Sentence*, Vol. 2, Indiana University Press, Bloomington–London 1975.

Danecki J., *Gramatyka języka arabskiego*, Vol. 1–2, Wydawnictwo Akademickie Dialog, Warszawa 2001.

Górska E., *Studium kontrastywne składni arabskich i polskich współczesnych tekstów literackich*, Wydawnictwo Uniwersytetu Jagiellońskiego, Kraków 2000.

Holes C., *Modern Arabic. Structures, Functions, and Varieties*, revised edition, Georgetown University Press, Washington 2004.

Lipiński E., *Semitic Languages Outline of a Comparative Grammar*, Peeters, Leuven 1997.

Polański K. (ed.), *Encyklopedia językoznawstwa ogólnego*, Zakład Narodowy im. Ossolińskich, Wrocław–Warszawa–Kraków 1993.

Ryding K.C., *A Reference Grammar of Modern Standard Arabic*, Cambridge University Press, Cambridge 2005.

Versteegh K. (ed.), *Encyclopedia of Arabic Language and Linguistics*, Vol. 1–5, Brill, Leiden–Boston 2006–2009.

Dictionaries

Baranov H.K., *Bolshoy arabsko-russkiy slovar*, Vol. 1–2, Moscow 2008.

Danecki J., Kozłowska J., *Słownik arabsko-polski*, Wiedza Powszechna, Warszawa 1996.

Wehr H., *A Dictionary of Modern Written Arabic*, Spoken Language Services, Münster–Ithaca–New York 1976.

Source texts

Al-Maḥādīn:

عبد الحميد المحادين، الخروج من العتمة: خمسون عاما لاستشراف الأفق، المؤسسة العربية للدراسات والنشر، بيروت 2003.

Šuqayr:

محمود شقير، مدن فاتنة وهواء طائش، المؤسسة العربية للدراسات والنشر، بيروت 2005.

Al-ʻAtīq:

فهد العتيق، كائن مؤجل، المؤسسة العربية للدراسات والنشر، بيروت 2005.

Al-Kayyālī:

نهلا خليل الكيالي، رحى الأيام، المؤسسة العربية للدراسات والنشر، بيروت 2005.

Nāṣir:

فتحية ناصر، الرجل السؤال، المؤسسة العربية للدراسات والنشر، بيروت 2009.

Al-Ahrām:

http://www.ahram.org.eg/

صحيفة مصرية يومية – 2010–2011

Aš-Šarq al-Awsaṭ:

http://www.aawsat.com/

جريدة العرب الدولية – 2010–2011

Al-Waṭan:

http://alwatan.kuwait.tt/

جريدة الوطن الإلكترونية – 2010–2011

BARBARA MICHALAK-PIKULSKA

Sultan Qaboos – image of the ruler in panegyrics and elegies by Omani poets

Accession to the throne of His Majesty Sultan Qaboos in 1970 was the real start of a new era in Oman. From the beginning Qaboos underlined that Omani people and their happiness are the most important for him. Qaboos was born on 18th November 1940 in Salalah as the only son of Sultan Sa'īd bin Taymūr and Sultana Mazūn bint Aḥmad al-Ma'shanī. He spend his first years of life in Salalah. When he turned sixteen, he went to England, where after a period of private education he joined the Royal Military Academy Sandhurst. After passing out from Sandhurst he spend a year with a British infantry battalion on tour duty in Germany. After returning to his homeland, he studied Islam and Oman's history in Salalah for six years.

After taking power, he encouraged the Omanis scattered around the world to return to their homeland and build a democratic state together. During the 50 years of his reign he built a strong, rich, stable and secure state. His visions with passion and conviction were implemented by the Omani people who have free access to health care, education and culture.

Over the past 50 years Oman has sought to develop friendly relations across the world. Sultan Qaboos offers the hand of friendship on a basis of mutual respect, non-interference in the internal affairs of other states. The Sultanate of Oman is a peace-loving country fortunate to have no problems with any other state. The Sultan himself was keen to promote peace, security and stability in Gulf and beyond.

Sultan Qaboos shares a unique bond with his subjects. From the beginning of his reign he took annual Royal Tours – annual trips around the country in order to get to know the inhabitants personally, their problems, needs and dreams. He learned first-hand on topics that concern the Omanis, and may even affect the future progress and prosperity of the Sultanate.

Qaboos enjoyed enormous authority all his life. He was always generous and made fair decisions. He put the Omani citizens first, and led Oman to flourish. His reign is considered a golden period in the history of the country.

The 1990s were already a full boom of Oman, both economic and socio-cultural. Citizens live in a beautiful and rich country perfectly managed by Sultan Qaboos. A whole host of poets appear in the literary arena, among which deserve attention: Sa'īd aṣ-Ṣaqlāwī, Sa'īda bint Khāṭir al-Fārisī, Turkiyya al-Būsa'īdī or Ṣāliḥ al-Fahdī. They all share a love for their country and its ruler, what they express in beautiful qaṣīdas. Panegyrics[1] written in honor of Sultan Qaboos are characterized by stylistic and thematic diversity, they are written in both colloquial language and dialect, as well as in a beautiful classic literary language. A full picture of the great ruler and patriotic feelings was inscribed in them that makes Sultan immortal, and the Omanis will always pursue his ideas. Sa'īda bint Khāṭir al-Fārisī (born in 1956) is a pioneer in literary and cultural activities in Oman. She is the author of such volumes of poetry as: *Madd fī baḥr al-a'māq* (The Tide in the Heart of the Sea) and *Ughniyāt li-ṭ-ṭufūla wa al-khuḍra* (Songs for Childhood and Greenery).

Sa'īda bint Khāṭir also wrote a panegyric *Anta nūr al-badr fīnā* (You are the Moonlight in Us) praising the Sultan. She considers him an outstanding leader who fulfills his mission with dedication and determination. He is loved by a nation that owes him a strong and secure state. Her feelings are authentic and at the same time represent the voice of a nation that enjoys peace and prosperity:

سعيدة بنت خاطر الفارسي

أنت نور البدر فينا

شمس الحضارة أشرقت

1 Panegyric (madīḥ) – "praise", "eulogy": generic terms that refer to panegyric poetry and the panegyric section of the qaṣīda. Panegyric is one of the oldest types of poetry: praise of gods, rulers, priests, chieftains, heroes, athletes and other figures is widespread throught the world's literatures, and panegyric occupies a central place in Arabic poetry. J.S. Meisami, P. Starkey (eds.), *Encyclopedia of Arabic Literature*, Vol. 2, Routledge, London–New York 1998, p. 482.

وبها عمان تزخرفت
قابوس طلّ بنوره
غمر المدائن والقرى
عم البلاد بخيره
الله أكبر جاءنا
قابوس يبني أمة
قابوس ينشئ دولة
قابوس سطر مجدنا
يسمو بنا
نحو العلا
ويعيد ماضي عزنا
بين الأمم[2]

You are the Moonlight in us
The sun of civilization has risen
And Oman has adorned itself with it.
Qaboos radiates his light
Has flooded town and village with his prosperity
. . .
God the greatest gave us
Qaboos who united the nation
Qaboos built the state
Qaboos has recorded our glory
He carries us
To the lofty height
And returns our former might
Amongst the nations

جئت يا قابوس نورا
وسرورا وحبورا
فاكتست
أرضي زهورا
أقحوانا
ياسمينا
لا تلمنا
لا تلمنا
ان لثمناكَ جبينا

2 Sa'īda bint Khāṭir al-Fārisī, *Anta nūr al-badr finā*, in: *Madd fī baḥr al-a'māq*, Muscat 1986, pp. 11–12.

لا تلم
دهرا رآنا
حاسداً إياك فينا
لا تلمنا
ان هتفنا
أنت فجرُ
أنت فخرُ
أنت نور البدر فينا
دمت قابوس المفدى
دمت سلطانا أمينا [3]

Qaboos, your arrival is light
It is joy and pleasure
Our land was covered with flowers
Camomile
Jasmine
Don't blame us
Don't blame
When we kiss your forehead
Don't blame
The Era that
is envious of you
Don't blame us
When we praise
You are the dawn
You are our pride
You are the light of the full moon among us
Persevere, Qaboos, dearest
Persevere as a reliable sultan

In a poem (nashīd) entitled *'Umān al-majd* (Glory to Oman) Sa'īda bint Khāṭir al-Fārisī speaks with love about his beloved homeland and its ruler. Refers to things related to the country, among others to a sail as a symbol of maritime power or incense – a symbol of nobility:

سعيدة بنت خاطر الفارسي
عمان المجد

[3] Ibid., pp. 24–25.

عمانُ مَجدُ أطلقَ الجَنَاحَا
شراعُ عَزْمٍ عَانَقَ الرياحَا
عمانُ نورٌ في العيونِ لاحا
عمانُ يا عطرَ اللُّبانِ فاحا
ألقاكِ في الشروقِ والأصيلِ
أهواكِ في عشقٍ وفي ذهولِ
*
قابوسُ نِعْمَ القائدُ الرشيدُ
وجيشُه الصقورُ والأسودُ
وشعبُه العقولُ والزنودُ
شعارُه الإصرارُ والصمودُ
صَحْوتُنا من فجرِه الجميلِ
نهضتُنا من عزمِه الجليلِ[4]

Glory to Oman

Oman *spread its wings*
The sail *firmly caught the wind*
Oman *is a glistening light in the eyes*
Oman *spreading the smell of incense*
I meet you *between dawn, late afternoon and sunset*
I love you *in love and amazement*
*
Qaboos *a great and sensible leader*
His army *is falcons and lions*
His people *are intelligence and forearm*
His motto *is determination and perseverance*
Our vigil *from His beautiful dawn*
Our rebirth *from his dignified firmness*

Turkiyya al-Būsa'īdī (born 1964) is also happy with the fact of living during the reign of Sultan Qaboos. She actively cooperated with the magazine *'Umāniyya*, and her poems often appear in the local press. She published the book *Liman aqūlu kalimātī* (To Whom Do These Words Speak?). Turkiyya addresses the topics of love, freedom, patriotism and national identity. Oman considers to be part of the great Arab nation (qawmiyya al-'arabiyya).[5]

---

4 Sa'īda bint Khāṭir al-Fārisī, *'Umān al-majd*, in: *Madd fī baḥr al-a'māq*, pp. 206–207.

5 Turkiyya al-Būsa'īdī, *Taṭwāf fī bilādī; Riḥlat musāfira*, in: *Liman aqūlu kalimātī*, Muscat 2000, pp. 125–127, 131–136.

In a poem *Anā 'Umāniyya* (I am Omani) from the volume *Anā imra'a istithnā'iyya* (I am an Exceptional Woman) she is proud of being an Omani:

تركية البوسعيدي
أنا عمانية
اسمي ,,تركية"
وبلادي عربية
أرضي خضراء
جناتي خضراء
وشموسي مشرقة وبهية
وبلادي عربية[6]

I am Omani
I am called Turkiyya
My country is Arab
My earth is green
My gardens are green
My suns always shine and are joyous
My country is Arab

Turkiyya al-Būsa'īdī in a poem (nashīd) entitled *'Umān . . 'Umān* expresses great love for her homeland. Oman is her home because her family lives here. She considers it the most beautiful country on earth and feels safe in it because it is ruled by a perfect ruler, whose name is even chirping by birds:

تركية البوسعيدي
عمان ... عمان
(1)
أهلاً .. أهلاً ..
أرض عمانْ
حُبك مكنونْ
في الوجدان
أهلاً .. أهلاً ..
أرض عمانْ
**

[6] Turkiyya al-Būsa'īdī, *Anā 'Umāniyya*, in: *Anā imra'a istithnā'iyya*, Muscat 1995/1996, p. 89.

(2)
الطير تغرد باسمك
فوق الأغصانْ
وتراثك حصن أمانْ
يا أجمل هذي الأوطانْ
يا أغلى ما في الدنيا
يا أرض .. عمانْ
**

(3)
في الحرب .. وفي السلم .. عمان
في كل الأزمان
يا جوهرة البلدان
يا نوراً في الأكوان
يا أرض عمانْ .... !!
***[7]

Oman... Oman

(1)
Welcome . . Welcome
Land of Oman
Love for you is sheltered
In conscience
Welcome . . Welcome
Land of Oman
**

(2)
The birds are chirping your name
On branches
And your heritage is a safe fortress
The most beautiful of all countries
The dearest in the world
Land of . . Oman
**

(3)
In war . . and peace . . Oman
In all Times
Oh, You the jewel of all countries
You are the light of the universe
Land of Oman . . . . !!
***

7 Ibid., pp. 97–100.

Ṣāliḥ al-Fahdī (born 1969 in Samā'il) is the author of the following volumes of poetry: *Hawājis* (Obsessions), *Mawāsim al-ghinā'* (The Seasons of Singing) and *Qābūs fī al-qalb* (Qaboos in Heart). They contain poems about love and patriotism, and the last one is dedicated to Sultan Qaboos on the occasion of the 30th anniversary of his assumption of power. Ṣāliḥ al-Fahdī referred with this volume to the rich tradition of Arabic poetry, especially the form of panegyric (maḍīḥ). The title poem *Qābūs fī al-qalb* (Qaboos in Heart) is distinguished by its structure compared to other poems from the volume because there are no rhymes or meter. The poet wanted to concentrate on the greatness of Sultan Qaboos, hence he did not want the form of the poem to become a limitation here:

صالح الفهدي
قابوس في القلب
أنت يا قابوس فيض الوعدِ
والشعب الوفي العهدِ
والوطن النضير السعدِ
كل المجدِ
كل المجد ،
كل المجدْ[8]

Qaboos in Heart
Oh Qaboos, you are full of promise
And You are faithfull to the covenant
And a flourishing happy homeland
(You are) all glory
All glory
All glory

The poem *Qābūs fī al-qalb* (Qaboos in Heart) consists of seven parts, and the content of each is worship and devotion to Sultan Qaboos, who devoted his entire life to Oman. The poet reveals his emotional attitude to the ruler of Oman and his homeland. On behalf of himself and the Omanis, he expresses his gratitude for his service to the country because it was his reign that led to its splendor. Ṣāliḥ al-Fahdī expresses his genuine joy and pride of being Omani.

---

8 Ṣāliḥ al-Fahdī, *Qābūs fī al-qalb*, in: *Qābūs fī al-qalb*, Muscat 2000, p. 23.

Poets often write typical panegyrics and elegies in the most popular meters used, i.e. al-basīṭ, al-kāmil, ar-ramal, and al-wāfir. Hymns and poems can be sung by using the ẖ abab meter (fa'ilun) in the form of taf'īla, e.g. in the poem *Ḥubb al-waṭan*[9] by Sa'īda bint Khāṭir al-Fārisī or in the poem *Anā 'Umāniyya* (I am an Omani) by Turkiyya al-Būsa'īdī .[10] We can also find song forms in the kāmil – majzū' meter in the poem *Qūlū lī-sulṭān al-bilād*[11] (Tell the Sultan of the Country) by Maḥmūd al-Khuṣaybī. Ṣāliḥ al-Fahdī in the poem *Khalīj*[12] (The Gulf) and Sa'īd aṣ-Ṣaqlāwī in the poem *Tawajjus*[13] (Apprehension) use the meter al-wāfir.[14]

After the death of Sultan Qaboos on January 10, 2020, a feeling of overwhelming emptiness remained in the nation. The pain remained intensified by every memory of the Sultan and the irreversible tragedy that struck Oman.

In the current globalized world, poetry found its place in the mass media: the Internet or the daily press, in which poems were published and voices of poets expressed the feelings of the Omani people. After the death of Sultan Qaboos one of the best modern poets Sa'īd aṣ-Ṣaqlāwī published the elegy, entitled *Yā sayyid al-ḥubb al-kabīr* (Oh Lord of Great Love), in honor of the ruler:

سعيد الصقلاوي

يا سيد الحب الكبير

وطن تسير على خطاك شموسه

وتزفه البركات نحو صعود

...

الله أودع فيك جنة حبه

ملأت شغاف عباده بمزيد[15]

[9] Sa'īda bint Khāṭir al-Fārisī, *Ḥubb al-waṭan*, in: *Ughniyāt li-ṭ-ṭufūla wa al-khuḍra*, Muscat 1988, p. 128.

[10] Turkiyya al-Būsa'īdī, *Anā 'Umāniyya*, in: *Anā imra'a istithnā'iyya*, p. 49.

[11] Maḥmūd al-Khuṣaybī, *Qūlū li-sulṭān al-bilād*, in: *Awrāq min shajarat al-majd*, Masqat 1987, pp. 107–108.

[12] Ṣāliḥ al-Fahdī, *Khalīj*, in: *Mawāsim al-ghinā'*, Muscat 1992, p. 15.

[13] Sa'īd aṣ-Ṣaqlāwī, *Tawajjus*, in: *The Awakening of the Moon. A Selection of Poems*, trans. A. Al-Shahham, M.V. Mcdonald, al-Batinah Printers, Muscat 1996, pp. 21–33.

[14] Ḥamīd bin 'Abd Allah bin Ḥamīd al-Jāmi'ī, *Rawḍat al-Albāb*, in: *Dīwān Abī Surūr*, Sama'il 1998, Vol. 1, p. 305.

[15] Sa'īd aṣ-Ṣaqlāwī, *Yā sayyid al-ḥubb al-kabīr*, "Al-Waṭan" (Muscat), 23rd January 2020, Vol. 49, No. 13204, p. 27.

Oh Lord of Great Love
Homeland suns are following your footsteps
Blessings bring Her to the top
. . .
God has placed in you a paradise of His love
You filled the hearts of people with even greater love

Another poem by Sa'īd aṣ-Ṣaqlāwī was entitled *Qarīban dā'iman tabqā* (You Will Always Be Close):

سعيد الصقلاوي
قريباً دائما تبقى
قريباً دائماً تبقى وحيّاً
وكل قلوبنا تدعو تنادي
حبيباً تسكن الأنفاسَ ورداً
ونفساً في اليقين وفي الرشادِ
ونهجكَ دائم الإشراق فينا
وحبكَ ملهمٌ روحَ البلادِ
أنا يا والدي أحياكَ ذِكْراً
وصوتكَ مالئٌ عينَ الفؤادِ[16]

You will always be Close
So close you will be and alive
In prayers, our hearts forbear
O' beloved dwelling our flowery breaths
Rightly guided by your affirm due care,
Your righteous pathway radiant and fair,
Your love inspiring the nation air,
O' my father I wholeheartedly carry your memories, I can't spare,
Your voice fulfilling me within I bear[17]

Among poets mourned the death of the Sultan Qaboos are also Hilāl bin Sayf ash-Shiyādī in the poem *Ansāka?* (Do I Forget You?) and Aḥmad bin Hilāl al-'Abrī in poem *Rāyat al-amjād* (Sign of Glory).

---

[16] Sa'īd aṣ-Ṣaqlāwī, *Qarīban dā'iman tabqā*, http://www.worldofculture2020.com/?p=1619 (3.08.2020).

[17] *You Will Always Be Close*, trans. Dr. Naimah Al-Ghamdi (Assistant Prof. in Imam Abdurahman Bin Faisal University KSA).

The poem *Ansāka?* (Do I Forget You?) in the form of *'amūdī* (meter *baḥr al-kāmil*, monorhyme *kāf maftūḥa* preceded by *alif*) was written by Hilāl bin Sayf ash-Shiyādī:

هلال بن سيف الشيادي
أنساك؟
قابوس يا حب العمانيين يا
عشق الزمان، عماننا تهواكا
حقا رحلت؟ فأنت حي بيننا
إني أراك هنا؛ ولست هناك
عذرا لكل الوقت ليس بوسعه
مهما تقادم فيّ أن أنساكا[18]

Do I forget you?
Oh Qaboos, Oh You adored by Omanis, Oh You
Beloved of time, our Oman loves you
Have you really gone? Since You are alive among us
I can see you here, and not there
I apologize to time, since as log as it will last
I will never be able to forget You

Traditional qaṣīda *'amūdī* (meter *baḥr al-wāfir*, monorhyme *rā' maftūḥa*) entitled *ad-Dars al-balīgh* (The meaningful lesson) was written by 'Abd al-Ḥalīm al-Badā'ī:

عبدالحليم البداعي
الدرس البليغ
وكم أصلحت بين خصوم أمس
فعاد الشر بعد الصلح خيرا
وكان السلم نهجك دون ضعف
وكنت بصالح الأقوام أدرى
فجنبت البلاد شرور حرب
تحيل بلادنا كفنا وقبرا
سنفخر دائما أبدا بأنا
شهدنا عصركم مذ كان فجرا[19]

---

[18] Hilāl bin Sayf ash-Shiyādī, *Ansāka?*, "Al-Waṭan" (Muscat), 20th January 2020, Vol. 49, No. (13201, Suppl. Culture and Art.

[19] 'Abd al-Ḥalīm al-Badā'ī, *ad-Dars al-balīgh*, "Al-Waṭan", 27th January 2020, Vol. 49, No. (13206), p. 23, Suppl. Culture and Art.

The meaningful lesson
Whenever you have reconciled old opponents
And after reconciliation, evil turned into good
Peace, not due to weakness, was Your path
You were the only one who knew best where their good was
You saved the homeland of the evil of war
That would make a country a coffin and a grave
We will be proud forever ever that
We've experienced your epoch since its dawn

Ahmad bin Hilal al-ʻAbrī has published the traditional qaṣīda *'amūdī* (meter *baḥr al-kāmil*, monorhyme *dāl maksūra* preceded by *alif*) entitled *Rāyat al-amjād* (Ensign of Fame):

أحمد بن هلال العبري
راية الأمجاد
يا ابنَ الكرامِ وأنجبتكَ كريمةٌ
(رجلُ الرجالِ وواحدُ الآحاد)
مَنْ يُشعِلُ الأضواءَ في عَتماتِنا
ويَرُشُّ ماءَ الحبِّ في الأحقاد
مَنْ أدرَكَتْ كلُّ الكواكبِ أنه
نجمُ النجومِ ورائدُ الرواد[20]

Ensign of Fame
Oh, noble son, you have a noble mother
(You are the truest man, you are the only one)
You are the one who lights in our darkness
And you sprinkle hatred with water of love
You are the One that all planets recognized
As a star of stars and a precursor of pioneers

The poets felt the need to open themselves to the world and express their despair after losing the closest person they considered Qaboos. They poured out their sorrows and shouted out despair, and their poems, which are memorable, are a source of reflection and emotion for every Omani

[20] Aḥmad bin Hilāl al-ʻAbrī in poem *Rāyat al-amjād*, "Al-Waṭan", 27th January 2020, Vol. 49, No. 13206, p. 23, Suppl. Culture and Art.

e.g. Shumaysa an-Nu'māniyya in her poem *Wadā'an yā abī* (Goodbye Father) writes:

شميسة النعمانية

وداعا يا أبي

أتى قابوسُ كي يشفي مُصابَ عمانَ
حتى استأنفَتْ أمجادها ..

. . .

مضى قابوسُ للغيماتِ
محمولاً على الأرواحِ.. في حُلَلٍ من المطرِ

. . .

هو الميزانْ
حامي السِّلْمِ قابوسٌ .. هو الحَرَسُ

. . .

هو السلطانُ قابوسٌ
سَمِيُّ النورِ
والتنورِ
والنُّوَّارِ
والتنويرِ في بلدي.. هو القبسُ هو القبسُ

. . .

فيا وجعي بهذا الحُزنِ..
إنَّ الحُزنَ سفَّاحٌ وفقدُكَ ليس يُحتملُ ..[21]

Goodbye Father

Qaboos has come to heal Oman of misfortunes,
Until the restoration of its glory . . .

. . .

Qaboos was heading for the clouds
Carried on souls . . . in a coat of rain

. . .

Qaboos is a balance
A protector and guardian of peace . . .

. . .

This is Sultan Qaboos
The Namesake of light,
And Fire,

---

[21] Shumaysa an-Nu'māniyya, *Wadā'an yā abī*, "Al-Waṭan", 28th January 2020, Vol. 50, No. 13207, p. 23, Suppl. Culture and Art.

And Flowering
And enlightenment in my country . . . He is a spark of light
. . .
Oh my pain in this sadness . . .
Sadness is deadly and the loss of You is unbearable

Poets appreciate in their poems Qaboos dedication to the country and to its citizens. They are sublime and constantly appear in them the name of the deceased because Sultan Qaboos was for them a man of a great spirit, for whom the most important thing was to serve the homeland, which is why His dedication was appreciated by the Omanis.

The first decades of reign of Sultan Qaboos are regarded as a period of intellectual modernization and reform. Social and cultural processes have started, opening new directions and possibilities while preserving and following their own traditions, history and culture.

The Poets describe the attitude of Omanis for whom the Homeland became the most important value following the rise to power of Qaboos. They emphasize his important role in stabilization of Sultanate.

Elegies[22] published after the death of Sultan Qaboos on January 10, 2020 were reminiscences. The virtues of the deceased were appreciated, thus providing another opportunity for the Omanis to express feelings of regret, sadness and tremendous pain. Together they mourned for the passing away of their beloved ruler.

References

‘Abd al-Ḥalīm al-Badā‘ī, *ad-Dars al-balīgh*, “Al-Waṭan”, 27th January 2020, Vol. 49, No. 13206, p. 23, Suppl. Culture and Art.

Aḥmad bin Hilāl al-‘Abrī in poem *Rāyat al-amjād*, “Al-Waṭan”, 27th January 2020, Vol. 49, No. 13206, p. 23, Suppl. Culture and Art.

Hilāl bin Sayf ash-Shiyādī, *Ansāka?*, “Al-Waṭan” (Muscat), 20th January 2020, Vol. 49, No. 13201, Suppl. Culture and Art.

[22] Elegy (rithā’ or marthiya) – the Arabic poetry of lamentation. The origin of this genre lay in pre-Islamic Arabia. Medieval Arab literary theorists have always closely associated the “rithā’ or marthiya” with the genre of “madīḥ” (panegyric). J.S. Meisami, P. Starkey, *Encyclopedia*..., pp. 663–664.

Maḥmūd al-Khuṣaybī, *Awrāq min shajarat al-majd*, Muscat 1987.

Meisami J.S., Starkey P. (eds.), *Encyclopedia of Arabic Literature*, Routledge, London–New York 1998.

Sa'īd aṣ-Ṣaqlāwī, *The Awakening of the Moon. A Selection of Poems*, trans. A. Al-Shahham, M.V. Mcdonald, al-Batinah Printers, Muscat 1996.

Sa'īd aṣ-Ṣaqlāwī, *Yā sayyid al-ḥubb al-kabīr*, "Al-Waṭan" (Muscat), 23rd January 2020, Vol. 49, No. (13204), p. 27.

Sa'īda bint Khāṭir al-Fārisī, *Madd fī baḥr al-a'māq*, Muscat 1986.

Sa'īda bint Khāṭir al-Fārisī, *Ḥubb al-waṭan*, in: *Ughniyāt li-ṭ-ṭufūla wa al-khuḍra*, Muscat 1988.

Ṣāliḥ al-Fahdī, *Mawāsim al-ghinā'*, Muscat 1992.

Ṣāliḥ al-Fahdī, *Qābūs fī al-qalb*, Muscat 2000.

Shumaysa an-Nu'māniyya, *Wadā'an yā abī*, "Al-Waṭan", 28th January 2020, Vol. 50, No. (13207), p. 23, Suppl. Culture and Art.

Turkiyya al-Būsa'īdī, *Anā 'Umāniyya*, in: *Anā imra'a istithnā'iyya*, Muscat 1995/1996.

Turkiyya al-Būsa'īdī, *Liman aqūlu kalimātī*, Muscat 2000.

YOUSEF SH'HADEH

Microfiction, flash fiction or very short story in modern Arabic literature

In the beginning of the 20th century, Arabic prose developed significantly, after moving away from the traditional writing patterns full of contrived rhymes and unnecessary structural decoration, which appears at the expense of meaning. The new literary genres differed and diversified, and as a result the traits of modern narrative forms became clear, especially the novel that began to acquire characteristics that distinguished it from the traditional story. The forms of story varied from long to medium, and from novella to a short story. A new type was formed in Arabic literature, defined with many names, the most prominent of which is "very short story", or flash fiction, usually between 100 to 1000 words in length.

Polish scholar Mariusz M. Leś took up this literary genre and its great spread in the digital age, although he mentions that critics ignore it: "Microfiction has many names. Basically, it is a very short narrative prose, very popular in the 'digital age', but mostly disrespected by critics".[1] The American expert on short stories, Catherine Sustana, enumerates the names of this type of prose as follows: "Flash fiction goes by many names, including microfiction, microstories, short-shorts, short short stories, very short stories, sudden fiction, postcard fiction, and nanofiction".[2]

---

1 M.M. Leś, *Flash fiction. Krótko o najkrótszych opowieściach*, in: D. Kulesza (ed.), *Tradycja i przyszłość genologii*, Wydawnictwo Uniwersytetu w Białymstoku, Białystok 2013, p. 203.

2 C. Sustana, *Flash Fiction Definition and History*, https://www.thoughtco.com/what-is-flash-fiction-2990523 (29.03.2020).

Since the 1970s, this narrative genre has begun to take a notable place in Arabic prose, which has been recognized by numerous critics and writers. However, as the Iraqi critic Bāsim 'Abd al-Ḥamīd Ḥammūdī asserts, the harbingers of the very short story in the Arab world occurred in 1930, when lawyer Nū'īl Rassām published his first stories, which represented the true beginning of this fictional art in Iraq.[3] A few years before that, the short story had emerged, about which the well-known Egyptian critic, Yūsuf ash-Shārūnī, said: "It is not possible to define one origin for it, because each era has its own narration, and every narrator has his own narration indeed..."[4]

The era of microfiction stories began to be a fact in the east of the Arab world and then reached the Maghreb countries. At the end of the 20th century and at the beginning of the 21st century, the authors of this type of prose, formed a large group of creators. This study focuses on examining and analysing various examples from the works of some writers, whose stories have expressed the extent of development of this new art, and its firmness as a literary genre clearly defined in modern Arab prose. The stories studied are samples of works written by authors from Mashreq and Maghreb, they are: Maḥmūd Shuqayr (Palestine), Ibrāhīm Darġūthī (Tunisia), and Muḥammad Ḥijjū (Morocco).

Before starting to study the works of these writers, the important question should be answered: Where did the flash fiction, as a genre of literature, come to Arabic prose? In fact, there has been a long debate regarding the origin of the very short story, whether it came from Europe, or did it arise as a result of natural development, or dramatic social, economic, and political changes that have occurred in Arab societies? Some researchers have claimed that great dramatic events, such as the defeat of the Arab armies during the war with Israel in June 1967, and the circumstances of the bitter Gulf War in 1991, formed a favourable climate for the advancement of this art.[5] Regardless of the difference of opinions regarding this issue, it is undeniable that the Arab microfiction writers are influenced by European literature, and are following its continuous achievements, and this may indicate that this genre of fiction has certainly come from Europe. Indeed,

---

3 Bāsim 'Abd al-Ḥamīd Ḥammūdī, *Riḥla ma'a al-qiṣṣa al-'irāqiyya*, Dār ar-Rashīd li-n-nashr, Baghdad 1980, p. 170.

4 Yūsuf ash-Shārūnī, *Dirāsāt fī al-qiṣṣa al-qaṣīra*, Dār Ṭalās li-d-dirāsāt wa an-nashr wa at-tarjama, Damascus 1989, p. 12.

5 Aḥmad Jāsim al-Ḥusayn, *Al-qiṣṣa al-qaṣīra jiddan... Muqāraba taḥlīliyya*, Dār at-Takwīn li-n-nashr, Damascus 2010, p. 146.

it cannot be ignored that most terms expressing *al-qiṣṣa al-qaṣīra jiddan* (very short story) are in harmony with the so-called microfiction stories, which appeared in European literature to refer to texts, which are determined by the number of their words, for example: *al-qiṣṣa al-wamḍa* (flash story), *al-qiṣṣa al-qaṣīra li-l-ġāya* (microstory), *al-qiṣṣa al-laqṭa* (sudden fiction), *al-qiṣṣa al-barqiyya* (postcard fiction).

It can be said that the first author who used the expression "a very short story" was Ernest Hemingway, writing a text, entitled *A Very Short Story* published in 1924.[6] A year later, this text was issued in the collection *In Our Time*,[7] but it was just a title, and the American writer did not intend to define it as a literary genre. It seems that the Arabic term came from that title of Hemingway's text precisely, and it is very much in harmony with the term: flash fiction story. However, it is not taken into account in the Arabic very short story to determine the exact number of words in the text, which may come in a few words, or may extend to more than one large page.

Upon examination of the studied works, which include texts published in Arabic by the Moroccan writer Muḥammad Ḥijjū, and other texts translated from Arabic into English, written by the Palestinian Maḥmūd Shuqayr and the Tunisian Ibrāhīm Darġūthī, it can be emphasized that they provide a good example of the Arabic very short story, in form and content completely.

It can be said that the stories written by Maḥmūd Shuqayr and Ibrāhīm Darġūthī do not pose any problems with the form, due to the authors' long experience in this field. It is no secret to researchers of Arabic literature that Shuqayr is one of the pioneers of this art in Palestine and the Arab Mashreq in general. However, Muḥammad Ḥijjū's experience in this field is still limited to publishing only one collection, but it embodies a distinct effort and an interesting example for this controversial literary genre. This collection is presented – according to its cover, under its main title – as "stories", and this raises some problems that require a sound and accurate approach to the issue of classifying the works within the literary genre to which they really belong.

The analysis of the texts of those three writers proves that they fulfil all the conditions, which are required by the rules of the art of very short story, or microfiction in general. In their construction and content, they

6 R. Scholes, *Decoding Papa: 'A Very Short Story' as Work and Text*, in: J.J. Benson (ed.), *New Critical Approaches to the Short Stories of Ernest Hemingway*, Duke University Press, Durham–London 1990, pp. 33–34.

7 E. Hemingway, *In Our Time: The 1924 Text*, University of Victoria, Canada 2015.

are in line with what might be called the "foundations" of this controversial literary genre, including those four pillars, which some Arab critics have identified as follows: "*al-qiṣaṣiyya* (storytelling), *al-jur'a* (audacity), *waḥdat al-fikra wa al-mawḍū'* (unity of thought and subject matter), and *at-takthīf* (intensification)".[8] For example, in terms of "storytelling", Muḥammad Ḥijjū recounts the events in an interesting narrative context, drawing in more than a hundred texts, very diverse characters, representing large segments of Moroccan society. The writer's audacity is manifested in the presentation of revolutionary ideas that fight religious and secular corruption and intellectual retardation. He presents confused characters, showing their weaknesses and strengths, and mocking their quirky behaviour and flawed attitudes towards negative phenomena and miserable social reality. Each text is usually represented as a narrative scene, concerned with one subject, where a series of thoughts is created that flow into one stream, and unite to serve a theme with specific purposes.

Muḥammad Ḥijjū does not adhere to a certain number of words, as his texts may be very short, ten words only, or may extend up till to reach a 150 words, but in all cases they do not increase more than that. The fact that the text is short does not mean that it is necessarily intensified, but in the very short stories of Ḥijjū's collection, titled *Rubbamā sawfa qad yakūnu* (Maybe It Will Be, Maybe), the intensification is inherent in all texts. The writer curbs the luxury of linguistic digressions and does not allow them to expand, and quickly turns to the event, and cuts off ideas that would lead to narrative sagging, or that might cause the topic to be fragmented. Most texts of the collection *Rubbamā sawfa qad yakūnu* are subtle, fun-wit, despite the dominant black scenes of the described reality, including the drawbacks of misery that the writer reveals. Sometimes, he mocks them, or denounces their ugliness, at other times. What is also noticed in these stories is that they are characterized by brevity in the number of words, the rapid movement of tense narration, charged with intense expressions full of suggestive and symbolic connotations, and remarkable language shifts and deviation. Besides, we clearly note the presence of paradoxes, wordplays, and metaphors that give the text of Muḥammad Ḥijjū a clever aesthetic flair. The writer picks his words very carefully, employing them skilfully even in the title, to the extent that they become semantic keys to his satirical texts. Perhaps this is what the reader realizes, from the moment he looks at the title of the collection, which may suggest a lot of humour or

---

8 Aḥmad Jāsim al-Ḥusayn, *Al-qiṣṣa al-qaṣīra…*, p. 43.

weirdness, and calls for a flood of questions, but all this ultimately leads to a peak of curiosity, which intensifies the pleasing suspense.

Muḥammad Ḥijjū often deals with everyday matters that may seem trivial, but makes them, with high artistic skills, great mysteries, which cause the reader to think deeply about them. The best example of this is a very short story, titled *Al-Luġz!* (The Mystery!), that draws us, in only two sentences, to contemplating a situation in which a man experiences every day. This man shaves his beard before eating breakfast, then goes to work, and there he finds that his facial hair has grown again. At the end of the text, the author leaves a provocative one word question: "Why…?"[9] Perhaps, through this question, he wants to invite us, as human beings, to reflect on our anxious life and its carefully drawn cycle, while we overlook it, preoccupied with our concerns and problems.

The very short story titled *Awlād 'Abd al-Wāḥid* (Sons of 'Abd al-Wāḥid) sarcastically criticizes selfish greedy people, who only care about their own interests, and concern to satisfy their insatiable desires, even at the expense of brotherhood. As for the principle followed in dealing with each other, it is based on mutual 'consent' and 'disregard': consent is for a while, and disregard extends up till achieving the goal. This principle reflects the embodiment of utilitarian and opportunistic relations, and the absence of sincere brotherly relations. The text may be understood through different interpretations, and this stems from the fact that the writer does not mean any particular person, or a certain group. He leaves the reader to perceive the text as he pleases, and return him to the negative phenomena present in all strata of society. One of the aesthetic characteristics of the text is the use of the name 'Abd al-Wāḥid as an ironic 'cipher', which refers the recipient to an enormous legacy of social implications, as well as their cultural and psychological connotations. The author confirms all this by repeating the word *wāḥid* (one) pointing to a part of the name of the title heroes, which comes at the ends of many phrases and sentences of the text. This word serves as a rhyme that deepens the connotations of the name and named by it persons, as well as their thought-provoking relationships. These interconnected bonds constitute thresholds for reflection, even since the beginning of the text. For example, the following sentence necessitates thinking about important hints to understand the troubled relations between the brothers heroes: „تنادى أولاد عبد **الواحد**، وهمهم **واحد**، أن يجتمعوا

[9] Muḥammad Ḥijjū, *Rubbamā sawfa qad yakūnu*, Al-Ha'ya al-Miṣriyya al-'Āmma li-l-Kitāb, Cairo 2017, p. 31.

"تحت سقف **واحد**، في زمن **واحد**، لمناقشة أمر **واحد**، فكل أمورهم ترد إلى أمر **واحد** (The sons of 'Abd al-**Wāḥid** called each other, because they have **one** concern, that to gather under **one** roof, at **one** time, in order to discuss **one** thing, for all their matters are related to **one** thing.).[10]

The contents of the collection *Rubbamā sawfa qad yakūnu* go beyond the borders of the Moroccan and the Arabic environment. They stem from the local, and extend to the global. In fact, the local topics of Muḥammad Ḥijjū's texts identify with the universal concerns, in terms of their humanitarian discourses. Here is the writer confirming in the story *Awlād 'Abd al-Wāḥid* (Sons of 'Abd al-Wāḥid) his comprehensive human approach, which perceives that the calamities and tragedies of people are the same in all this world, even if the reasons differ. He moves from ridiculous irony to a serious topic that refers to the tragedies of wars and the suffering of people regardless of their nationalities:

> And since the consensual approach requires a large portion of disregard, the sons of Abdel Wahid agreed to share the cake, the bowl, the she-mule, the skin of the ewe, the pallor of shoes, the ant's feathers, the mosquito's breath . . . Palestine's tears, Bosnia's groans, and the sorrows of Syria and Andalusia, even if there is a disparity between each one.[11]

In a very short story, titled *Al-'Aqīqa* (The Oblation), Muḥammad Ḥijjū highlights some of the customs and traditions of Moroccan society, which may not be bad, but their use by clerics to be an occasion for devouring hearty meals, and for inventing fatwas, makes it unacceptable. The title refers to the carcass that is sacrificed to a newborn when his hair is shaved, on the seventh day of birth. It appears that the religious exploitation of this social tradition has urged the author to write a text that displays this exacerbating phenomenon in Moroccan Muslim society. It is a satirical text that employs language skilfully to suit its comic character. It is noticed that the writer uses rhymes to increase the influence in creating a scene similar to the atmosphere of religious sermons, which offer artificial speech at the expense of meaning:

> In all times
> They sat at the table. The food has brought.

[10] Ibid., p. 41.
[11] Ibid.

> He came close and said: "In the name of God, the Most Gracious, the Most Merciful", then quickly began swallowing.
>
> After eating the fruits, he retracted to the pad and belched.
>
> He relaxed, freed from his turban. His hair was thick and the brain was bald.[12]

Muḥammad Ḥijjū relies in his texts on the verbal similarity between certain words, so he uses them proficiently in an effort to show that language is the main element in the narrative process that offers pleasure, humour, and suspense. Of note, the writer sought to employ grammar and syntax in his texts in a satirical, cheerful, and comical style. A good example is the following very short stories: *I'rāb al-ḥāl* (The Syntax of Case), *Inna wa nazawātuhā* ('That' and its Whims), *Qāba Qawsayn* (Close to Brackets), and *Aḍ-Ḍamāi'r al-muttaṣila* (Possessive Pronouns). Attention is also drawn by a text, titled *Al-I'rāb al-muwaḥḥad* (Unified Syntax), in which the author mocks an opportunist by using the grammatical cases in an interesting and innovative way. Moreover, the Moroccan writer replaces some letters of words with other letters that distort their pronunciation, as if he wanted to highlight the distortion of that opportunist, not only verbally, but also psychologically, which suggests that he is an abnormal person. For example, the letter *rā'* (*r*) is replaced by the letters *lām* (*l*), *dāl* (*d*), and *tā'* (*t*), as in the following words: *yalkabu* or *yadkabu*, should be *yarkabu* (he rides); *qiṭāl* or *qiṭāt*, should be *qiṭār* (train); *muḍāli'*, should be *muḍāri'* (present); *malfū'* or *madfū'*, should be *marfū'* (nominative); *majlūl* or *majdūd*, should be *majrūr* (genitive).[13]

It can be said that the Moroccan writer delights in mixing the words of his texts with grammatical terms, and this mixing does not come arbitrarily, but rather it carries certain hints and indications that make the sentences enigmatic, or more precisely, that includes several interpretations. If we look closely at the very short story *I'rāb al-ḥāl*, we would find that the interpretations of the text extend beyond the meanings that are generated from grammatical cases. Moreover, Muḥammad Ḥijjū insists, at times, to break the logic of linguistic order, so we find him using verbs in past tense instead of the future tense, and verbs in present and future tenses instead of the past tense. Breaking these grammatical rules indicates the irrational surreal reality, which the writer wants to destroy, as he realizes its great

12 Ibid., p. 30.
13 Ibid., p. 45.

influence on the life of a human who has lost the basics of decent living. Perhaps this is what suggests a very short story, titled *Khayār* (Option):

> We came out tomorrow, we want 'what'.
> We found what we wanted, and we found no trace of 'what',
> Or maybe we will find what we want yesterday, or we may not find a trace of 'what'.
> You, and we, are at one option.[14]

The intense repetition of certain synonymous words is remarkable in the text, titled *Al-Qarḍ al-la'īn* (Damned Loan), and it comes in harmony with the description of the borrower's condition, so that a long context is formed that includes even twelve synonymous verbs in one sentence: *yaṭlu-bu* (ask), *yarġabu* (desire), *yashā'u* (want), *yawaddu*, (would like) *ya'mulu* (hope), etc. This deliberate repetition, of those synonyms, is a smart way to emphasize the borrower's urgent need to keep his parliamentary position, until the dreaded loan is paid off. The repetition of the phrase "even for a while" suggests important indications, referring to the aggravating anxiety in the psyche of the hero, who realises the importance of time, and the danger of exceeding its limits, in the battle of repaying the severe loan. What attracts attention in this text is that the narrator speaks about and the bank a woman, supposed to be his wife, in one sentence, but he does not mention the woman by name, and only puts a feminine pronoun, which we do not know who specifically represents: "In order to provide the bank, at the end of every month, with what her fat mouth filled with".[15] It can be said here, that the writer alludes to the reader and suggests to him that the bank is like a woman, or that the hero's woman is like a bank, asking her debt-ridden husband more and more money:

> He bought himself and his family a big house,
> For this purpose he borrowed a lot of money from the bank,
> And if he loses the parliamentary position, he will lose remuneration,
> He will have a curse in the ends of months, he will not be able to provide the instalments.
> For this, he asks, longings, wants, wishes, would like, hopes, seeks, aims, aspires, requests, begs and dreams of keeping the position, even for a while,

---

[14] Ibid., p. 15.
[15] Ibid., p. 103.

In order to provide the bank, at the end of every month, with what her fat mouth filled with.

Signing: Even for a while.[16]

Reading Ibrāhīm Darġūthī's microfiction stories, it could be seen that they contain the four pillars of the very short story: *al-qiṣaṣiyya* (storytelling), *al-jur'a* (audacity), *waḥdat al-fikra wa al-mawḍū'* (unity of thought and subject matter), and *at-takthīf* (intensification). In the text, entitled *Al-Mu'taqal* (The Detention), Darġūthī presents a current topic that requires boldness to write, and depicts a dangerous aspect of reality in the Arab world, which revolves around the brutal killing of prisoners. The reader does not know who is the executing party, is it a state or terrorist organization, and does not know who is the victim and the reason for the arrest. However, there are indications that the implementing body has a "military police", and it has prisons and execution grounds. It turns out that the digression in the narrative process is not the author's goal, and the details are not desirable in this intensifying atmosphere of the text. The important thing here is to surprise the reader and generate shock to him when reading the last line that contains the scene of the butcher cutting off the heads of prisoners, mentioning the name of God. This scene may look surreal, but it does not move away from the reality in which religion is exploited and killing becomes as if it were the obligations of religion.

In a few lines, the text of Ibrāhīm Darġūthī narrates a great tragedy experienced by the oppressed peoples ruled by military dictatorship and deadly religious extremism. In a few words, the author draws scenes that can be expanded much more than they are, but the form used here, which is a very short story, is sufficient to convey the idea that the Tunisian writer wanted:

> Pounding the ground of the detention with their heavy boots at dawn, the guards came in. Before opening the door, he had woken up and sat rubbing his eyes with his two hands that were almost frozen because of coldness. The chief guard asked him to stand up and so did he. The military police walked forward while he, gloomily, followed them. When they reached the execution hall, he saw groups of prisoners. Their hands and legs were tied up with thick folds on their eyes.
>
> He said to himself:

[16] Ibid., pp. 102–103.

> – There are so many in this rainy day.
>
> He did not add any word as he got used to this kind of work. The chief guard handed him his shining sharp knife. He started to slaughter them one by one while murmuring the name of Allah with each head that he cut.[17]

It can be said that Maḥmūd Shuqayr's texts also include the four pillars, which characterize the genre of the very short story. They usually contain a few words, and their suggestive indirect ends are open, incomprehensible in one sense, and require the reader to think about their intentions. The flash fiction story, entitled *Waḥda* (Solitude), can be a good example of the method used by the Palestinian writer to present his thoughts and messages through the very short story. The author portrays an important aspect of the life of a man who feels lonely and desperate, thus we see him treating his cat like a woman. It seems that the writer wants to say that the heightened sense of loneliness leads to a separation of man from reality, and makes him live in illusion and confusion:

> Shortly after midnight, he was awakened by the stingingly cold air. He walked to the window, reprimanding himself for forgetting to close it before going to bed.
>
> He went back to bed. He stopped when he noticed that the cat was not on his bed. She was not sitting in the corner nor was she stretched out under the aging table.
>
> He went to the window again and waited. When despair finally caught up with him, he secluded himself in his bed. "How many times have I warned her not to go out at night?!" he mumbled and coughed, as if speaking about a woman.[18]

The very short stories of Ibrāhīm Darġūthī are characterized by intensification, which is noticeably reflected in the narration and sentence structure. The best example of this is the text entitled *Al-'Aqrab* (Scorpion), where we see the sentences concise and suggestive, and the rhythm dynamically leads to a quick end causing shock to the recipient. It must be pointed out here that this tense narrative form and artistic style that depends on the

---

[17] Ibrāhīm Darġūthī, *Under Warm Sun*, in: *Taḥta samā' dāfi'a*, trans. H. Hegazy, Ad-Dār ath-Thaqāfiyya li-n-nashr wa at-tawzī', Tunis 2014, p. 34.

[18] Maḥmūd Shuqayr, *Ṭuqūs li-l-mar'a ash-shaqiyya*, trans. Fadwā al-Qāsim, Dār ibn Rushd, Amman 1986, p. 15.

shock perfectly fits the subject of the story and its psychologically tense hero. In many cases, psychological tension causes a person to act as a blind person, to lose wisdom, and as a result he lives in an illusion and imagines unrealistic things to happen:

> He stood in front of the door more than one time. The fearful insect was flying in the air before landing on his shoulders like melted lead. He left the door half-opened and entered. He put his television on, then put it off after a minute. He put a tape in his recorder, but ejected it before the start of the music. Lying on his bed, he closed his eyes, and all in sudden he stood up. He made his way to the wall and hit the awful insect with all his fist. The pain that rose in his arm, under his watch wrist, was unbearable. It hurt him continuously, stopped for a moment then erupted more painfully. He scratched his arm until the blood dripped. The arm swelled. He then turned to the wall hitting it again and again, but his strength failed him.
>
> On falling beside the wall, he whispered:
>
> – How awful is this sting of that terrible scorpion…![19]

Although the texts of Muḥammad Ḥijjū are characterized by noticeable intensification, shortness and a limited number of words, they open up to poetry to intertextualize with some poems to serve the idea presented. We find that the writer, at the beginning, deals with poetry in its linguistic shifts and changes its expressions, creating surprise, or slight shock, through the paradoxes generated by the quotes. Among this is intertwining with two verses of poetry by Ibn Ġayyāth an-Najdī, which are very similar to two verses attributed to ʿAlī ibn Abī Ṭālib. These two quoted lines play an important role in the very short story titled *Ḥubb al-anābīb* (Love of Pipes), in terms of affirming the impossibility of the return of serenity in emotional relationships, after experiencing the disappointment or betrayal of the beloved:

> He told her in the first month of the time of passion, love and wisdom:
>
> Be sure to keep the hearts out of grief, because it is difficult to serenity them after chagrin
>
> Hearts, if they are free of feelings of love, would be like a broken bottle that cannot be fixed.[20]

---

19 Ibrāhīm Darġūthī, *Under…*, p. 37.
20 Muḥammad Ḥijjū, *Rubbamā…*, p. 9.

The very short story, *Ġadr az-zaman* (Treachery of Time) by Muḥammad Ḥijjū, intertextualizes with the famous poem *Rithā' al-Andalus* (Elegy for al-Andalus) written by Abū al-Baqā' Ṣāliḥ ar-Rundī (1204–1285), using words and phrases from it, the most important of which is the word *zman* (time). The phrase, quoted by the Moroccan writer, is taken from the beginning of Ar-Rundī's poem: "لكل شيء إذا ما تمَ نقصانُ... فلا يُغرّ بطيب العيش إنسانُ"[21] (Everything declines after reaching perfection, therefore let no man be beguiled by the sweetness of a pleasant life).[22] But Muḥammad Ḥijjū replaces the word *insān* (human) with *ġaflān* (oblivious) that suits the semantic content of the poetic verse and adds a comic flair to it, and it also corresponds fully to the rhyme and metre. Ḥijjū humanizes time to become mortal like a human being, and to be changed whenever places differ, which the author points to the extent of their distance according to a semantic linguistic perspective, through which the differences between the used words appear: *hunā* (here), *hunāka* (there), and *hunālika* (over there). Humanization may form – as Hussein says – "to provide the text with distinctive semantic allusions, and to give it some humour".[23] Humour can be felt through the use of humanized time by the Moroccan writer. In addition, the visual drawing of the text words increases the wittiness, and makes it consistent with its implications in the process of showing the extent of proximity and distance spatially and temporally:

> I saw him . . . I swear I saw him. His nose was here. He lived for a while and became here. Then he lived another time, and he became
> Here, after a while
> Here, then
> Here, then
> There is, then
> Over there
> Time varies from one period to another . . . therefore let no oblivious man be beguiled by the sweetness of a pleasant life.[24]

---

21 See: Muḥammad Ruḍwān ad-Dāya, *Abū al-Baqā' ar-Rundī Shā'ir al-Andalus*, 'Ālam al-Kutub li-ṭ-Ṭibā'a wa an-nashr wa at-tawzī', Beirut 1986.

22 J.T. Monroe, *Hispano-Arabic Poetry – a Student Anthology*, University of California Press, Berkeley–Los Angeles–London 1974, pp. 332–334.

23 Aḥmad Jāsim al-Ḥusayn, *Al-qiṣṣa al-qaṣīra as-sūriyya wa naqduhā fī al-qarn al-'ishrīn*, Ittihād al-Kuttāb al-'Arab, Damascus 2001, p. 333.

24 Muḥammad Ḥijjū, *Rubbamā...*, p. 23.

Muḥammad Ḥijjū deals with phrases he quotes from literary texts that slightly alter it, and makes it the focus of intertextuality, which gives his narration a pleasant flavour, especially since most of those quotes used to be heard by the Arab ear. These expressions are popular because they are sung, such as the poem *Qāri'at al-funjān* (The Coffee Cup Reader), by Nizār Qabbānī, whose words are included in the very short story *Sījāra wa funjān* (A Cigarette and a Cup). Muḥammad Ḥijjū writes: "She sat down, with tobacco in her hand and the lighter… pondering the cup, the cup of spilled tea. We cannot distinguish, it may be a cup of coffee. But it is certainly not upside down".[25] When a Arab reads this text, he automatically recalls in his mind Qabbānī's poem, which was a widespread song: "She sat down, with the fear in her eyes… Pondering my upside down cup…"[26] In this way, Muḥammad Ḥijjū succeeds in drawing the recipient to think, and making him invoke the comparisons through humorous paradoxes.

Sometimes, intertextuality comes in the stories of Muḥammad Ḥijjū in the form of quotes from poetry, which the writer turns into a prose sentence, as in the story *Khabar Kāna* (Predicative Situation), where he quotes phrases from a poem, titled *Al-Wadā'* (Farewell), by Ibrāhīm Nājī, which was sang by legendary Egyptian singer Umm Kulthūm, under the title *Al-Aṭlāl* (Ruins):

> Has love ever seen drunk people like us?
> How much imagination we built around us
> And walked in a moonlit road,
> where joy jumped before us
> We laughed like two little kids together,
> and we ran till we outrun our shadow![27]

Muḥammad Ḥijjū makes these poetic phrases, which are memorized by many generations of Arabs, as a prose text that serves his artistic vision. It can be said that the writer aims to inform the reader that the era of joyful romanticism will not return, even if the beautiful past returns. Muḥammad Ḥijjū concludes his very short story with words smelling sarcasm, and strangeness that gives the text a wit, reinforced by a realistic indication dazzled by the shock of the incredible:

---

[25] Ibid., p. 34.

[26] Nizār Qabbānī, *Qaṣā'id mutawaḥḥisha*, Manshūrāt Nizār Qabbānī, Beirut 1970, p. 4.

[27] Ibrāhīm Nājī, *Al-A'māl al-Kāmila*, 3rd ed., Dār ash-Shurūq, Cairo 1996, pp. 416–417.

> My joy heard that the next year had passed and no longer existed, and myself told me: Let's wait the last year; when it will return, we will be young, then we'll laugh like two little kids together, and run till we precede our shadows . . . Love will never see drunk people like us.
>
> I got to know myself, we exchanged greetings and best wishes for the Eid, and we went ahead waiting the last year.[28]

In the very short story, entitled *Ṭalāq* (Divorce), by Ibrāhīm Darġūthī, intertextuality is not literal quotations, but rather suggestive thoughts in the form of cute allusions that take us from modern time to the eighth century, through the theme of love. Perhaps the author's message in this text seeks to emphasize that love in contemporary life is no longer real, as it often dies after marriage, and therefore divorce is widespread. Love is no longer immortal and perfect as it was in the past, in the famous story which heroes are Buthayna and the poet Jamīl ibn 'Abd Allāh ibn Ma'mar al-'Udhrī, also known as Jamil Buthaina. Keywords can be set for Darġūthī's text as follows: poet, love, beloved, Jamil, Buthaina. The author uses these words to emphasize the big difference between the contemporary poet who is characterized by betrayal and lies, and the poet of the past centuries, the honest and loyal to his beloved until death. At the end of the text, the author leaves notes on the story of Jamil Buthaina to remind the reader of the extent to which life's values have changed, in the forefront of which is love that has changed with time:

> The judge begged the man and the women who sat before him:
>
> – Please take decision, this is the last session for reconciliation, and as you know that the worst available thing in our religion is divorce.
>
> He said:
>
> – Your honour, please put an end to this case now.
>
> I will pay this woman a big dowry on one condition… let me take and bring up the kids. This is the greatest disaster that God imposed upon his wretch miserable servant.
>
> She said:
>
> – Sorry, sir. I refuse his big dowry, and I won't live with him anymore. I want everyone to his lies to, present or absent, he was not honest even one day. He betrays me every time. He is, sir, a poet. Do poets tell truth, sir?

---

28 Muḥammad Ḥijjū, *Rubbamā...*, p. 45.

– He is, sir, my pain in this mortal life, I do not know what kind of pain I will face in the Doomsday? Is there anything worse than living with a bad man like this?

Next day, all papers wrote about the divorce of the century and the first pages were ornamented with the photos of: Jamil and Buthaina.

P.S. Jamil was a poet lived in the eighth century.

Buthaina: his beloved.

They lived a great love story in that immemorial time.[29]

In some titles and narrative text of his very short stories, Muḥammad Ḥijjū uses words and phrases well-known literary works, in order to attract the attention of the reader, and make him think about the intention of using them, until he reaches a convincing interpretation of the messages hidden in them. Often times, those messages are vague, so we need to decode them. For example, we find titles adapted from famous works, such as: *Mawsim al-Hijra ilā ash-Shamāl* (Season of Migration to the North) by Aṭ-Ṭayyib Ṣāliḥ (Tayeb Salih), and *Thartharah fawqa an-Nīl* (Adrift on the Nile) by Najīb Maḥfūẓ (Naguib Mahfouz), which Ḥijjū turns provocatively into *Thartharah fawqa az-zift* (Adrift on the Asphalt). The author of *Rubbamā sawfa qad yakūnu* (Maybe It Will Be, Maybe) uses *Al-Khīmyā'ī* (The Alchemist) and *Ash-Shaykh wa al-baḥr* (The Old Man and the Sea) as titles of two of his texts, which are the same titles of the well-known novels written by the Brazilian Paulo Coelho and the American Ernest Hemingway. However, quoting the title words does not only come from literary works, but also from recognised names and phenomena. For example, the text, entitled *Muthallath Kanūdā* (Kanūdā Triangle) suggests, at first sight, the famous Bermuda Triangle. In light of this, the reader should strive to understand what the writer means by *Kanūdā* that does not correspond to the Arabic semantics, although a similar word *Kanūdā*[30] appears in the Holy Qur'an, but in a different meaning – "ungrateful" as follows: "Indeed, the human being is ungrateful to his Lord".[31] It can be asked here: Did the writer want, through playing with words, formed by "Bermuda" and *Kanūdā*, to link the famous Triangle with the "triangle" of evil lying within man,

[29] Ibrāhīm Darġūthī, *Under...*, p. 47.

[30] Some meanings of this word mentioned by Ibn Manẓūr: ungrateful, disbelieving, blaming his Lord counting misfortunes and forgetting blessings. See: Muḥammad ibn Mukarram ibn Manẓūr, *Lisān al-'Arab*, Vol. 3, Dār Ṣādir, Beirut 1994, p. 381.

[31] *The Quran* [18:16], trans. Talal Itani, ClearQuran, Dallas–Beirut 2012.

who reaps nothing but regret? Perhaps reading the text in light of this interpretation, one can find justification acceptable to the reader:

> You want crops,
> Or a harvest that a reaper does not envy?
> Yes, and what do I plant?
> Plant the goodness
> What do I reap?
> Regret.
> only?
> ...![32]

Very short story authors often resort to puzzles or put a mysterious sentence at the end of the text, the significance of which cannot be understood with specific interpretation. Perhaps the aim of these writers is to make the text open to many interpretations, allowing the recipient to reflect and look at the text not from one side, but from several angles. In the story entitled *Al-Mā'ida* (The Table), Ibrāhīm Darġūthī follows this method, leaving the last sentence without clarification. The woman, who is waiting for her husband to return home after completing his night work, opens the door and sees "the comer, who has forgotten his way back". Here, the question about the identity of that comer appears necessary, is he the husband? If so, then why did he forget his way back! It is clear here that Darġūthī writes a realistic story that depicts the Tunisian woman who is patient, faithful, and loyal to her husband, who always carries out her duties as a smiling and satisfied wife. The author also provides a realistic picture of the industrious Tunisian miner who works at night for his livelihood. Therefore, if the end of the story was not with that mysterious sentence, the text would be an ordinary real picture of the life of the hard workers, and there would be nothing surprising or contemplative:

> When the muezzin starts saying: "Prayer is better than sleep, oh servants of God", she gets up at once and stands up. She washes and prays. Then she goes to the kitchen to make coffee and puts water on fire. This is necessary for him to take his shower on his return from the night shift at the phosphate mine.

---

[32] Muḥammad Ḥijjū, *Rubbamā...*, p. 8.

> By six she must have finished her daily routines, to start setting the table. She chooses cups and clean them carefully to look more bright. Then she goes to the bath to check the towel, the sink, and the soap, then looks at the fumes ascending from hot water bucket. She smiles contently. Then she returns to the table until the mines alarm rings aloud, calling at the team of morning shift. She opens the door for the comer, from the heart of the mountain, who has forgotten his way back… his way home…![33]

In the short-short story, titled *Iftiqād* (Loss), Maḥmūd Shuqayr presents a text that is enigmatic and full of symbols, so the reader will not be able to decipher it without carefully examining every word in it. The story is simple, telling about two lovers who are convinced they will lose each other one day. But the simplicity of the topic does not mean the ease of understanding its symbolism, which can be viewed from a comprehensive human perspective, and also from the perspective of a specific Palestinian reality. There are some hints that should be perceived symbolically, for example, the heroine will lose her lover one evening (this is a symbol that he had bid farewell to her in the hope of returning to her in the evening), and he will lose her one morning (this indicates that he knows that he will lose his freedom in the morning, because Palestinian homes are often raided by the Israeli Army in the morning). What confirms the expectation of the arrest of the hero is that "he'd be prohibited from frequenting places and traversing long distances", and this suggests that he will be arrested at any moment, as he is under occupation. At the end of the story, the heroine arrives at his home and finds it empty and dark. This is an indication that the hero may have been arrested, and all this falls within the symbolism of the Palestinian reality under occupation.

In fact, the text has no direct word on Palestinian reality or arrest, so the story can be understood quite differently. If a non-Palestinian person reads it, he may have other interpretations that are far from the Palestinian reality. In conclusion, the text is open and presents a comprehensive human topic of absence and loss:

> She knew, from the moment he gave her that story about the lover who went absent, she'd lose him some evening. She'd look for him at home, in the streets, in all the places he often visited. And she knew she wouldn't stumble on an answer.

[33] Ibrāhīm Darġūthī, *Under…*, p. 55.

> He knew he'd lose her one morning; that he wouldn't be able to look for her because he'd be prohibited from frequenting places and traversing long distances.
>
> One day, she received mysterious news. She ran like a filly till she reached his distant home. She dared not enter; the house was haunted by silence and a thick condensation of darkness coated its walls.[34]

Maḥmūd Shuqayr's very short stories, in general, deal with topics of a humanitarian nature, and highlight the suffering of people, especially the poor among them. In the text, titled *Ashyā'* (Things), the Palestinian writer presents a scene expressing the reality of the crushed poor class, generally summarizing the situation of the poor, whose income is limited. The author here presents an image of a woman who is caring for her children, but her salary is barely sufficient to cover living and school expenses and education. She used to buy medicines regularly "for the man who's been sleeping in the house for years", but the author does not give any information about this person. So we do not know whether he is her husband, nor do we know his fate, and what happened to him. The only obvious thing is that this woman manages the family's affairs alone, and she does not receive any assistance from any party.

Of course, it is possible to understand the story as depicting a part of the Palestinian reality under occupation, as there are no state institutions that provide financial assistance to children, and in the absence of the husband, it is the Palestinian woman who supports the children in all respects. The heroine of this story represents the poor mother who is dedicated to caring for her children, and she rarely takes care of herself and her beauty. When she buys a cheap perfume from a box on the sidewalk, and the seller appears blind, the reader realizes the misery that the writer points to. The blind seller behind his box perpetuates the image of extreme poverty, which is consistent with the author's message in shedding light on the lives of the poor – the buyer and the seller:

> Nothing left from her meagre salary. As usual every month, she bought medicines for the man who's been sleeping in the house for years. She bought the school uniform for the girl and a pair of trousers to wear underneath. She bought candy and notebooks for the children. With what she had left, and for the first time in age, she bought herself eye-liner, powder, and perfumes

---

[34] Maḥmūd Shuqayr, *Ṭuqūs...*, p. 18.

> with some kind of scent or another, from a blind street vendor sitting on his haunches behind his glass box.[35]

Microfiction gives the author the opportunity to present shots and quick scenes that evoke the reader's sympathy and human feelings. In his very short story, entitled *Umūma* (Motherhood), Ibrāhīm Darġūthī deals with the issue of motherhood, but not that, which women experience, and not that, which everyone knows its existential importance. It is the animal maternity that the writer provides coupled with the issue of mother's sacrifice for her children. The narration focuses on an intensive description of the sight of an ordinary dog with no name, and nothing in it that distinguishes it from others. The story is generally not characterized by specific events, but its content revolves around one idea the writer wanted to confirm, which is an extremely important existential fact: that the mother dies in order for her young children to live. Here, it can be said that Ibrāhīm Darġūthī wanted to emphasize that motherhood in animals is not different from motherhood in humans. Mother is always ready to sacrifice for the sake of her children, and they also cling to her as she is the source of life. She gives them life even when she dies:

> Lying on her left side feeding her juniors,
>
> I saw her in the evening.
>
> Her eyes, looked like honey in its bright colour, wide-open, and all her five cubs were feeding from her bosom and happily played with their little claws against each other.
>
> It was our beloved dog.
>
> Only the mother dog slept on left side.
>
> Our female dog who had no name, used to run ahead in front of my father to our field and to return before night, howling at every stranger, and was very pleased with every friend. She kept awake by the farm, on winter and summer.
>
> In the morning I saw her on her left shoulder feeding her juniors as usual.
>
> Groups of green flies were hovering round her.
>
> I came near to take one. The milk dripped from his mouth, and he rumbled.
>
> I dropped him, he went back to the bosom for the milk.
>
> I lifted him up again, the milk poured from the muzzle once more.
>
> The green flies buzzed, but then they landed on the dead dog.[36]

---

35 Ibid., p. 26.

36 Ibrāhīm Darġūthī, *Under...*, p. 36.

In the very short story, entitled *Ḥirmān* (Deprivation), Maḥmūd Shuqayr deals with the issue of motherhood in a different way than the Tunisian writer. Shuqayr focuses on the great impact on a child's psyche upon losing a mother. The narrator does not explain how and why the mother died, this is not important, the text is short, and embodies a scene that is not strange in people's lives. The important thing here is the infant's behaviour and the effect of the mother's disappearance on his life, so the author highlights the little child who touches his mother's chest in search of the breast. Here we feel that the bosom of the mother is the life itself and safety for the child, and when he loses it, he falls into deprivation, crying and disappointment, and this will have an impact on his future life:

> The baby who awoke in the dusty morning didn't want to wake his mother from her heavy sleep. There he sat, next to her on the bed, contemplating her calm face, as still as water.
>
> The baby who awoke early felt hungry. He leaned toward his mother, in an attempt to take her out breast, but his tiny hands failed him.
>
> The baby threw himself in the lap of tears. People came from everywhere and gathered in the house. They wept inside the house for a while, and then they carried the baby's mother to a place he does not know to this day.[37]

The universal human concern is overwhelmed in Ibrāhīm Darġūthī's microfiction stories, where we see that human suffering becomes one in countries of emigration. Difficult working conditions, changing the environment and climate, and moving away from the motherland and the family make the immigrant anxious, frustrated and tired. In a very short story, entitled *Al-Banġālī* (The Bengali), the Tunisian writer presents a dramatic scene that summarizes the lives of immigrants from different countries seeking work in the Arab Gulf countries. In short sentences, Darġūthī shows similar feelings and suffering among people, regardless of their nationalities. There is no doubt that the last sentence clearly shows that the feeling of alienation brings immigrants together, and makes them sympathize with each other:

> He, at once, entered after me into the bed room at King Faisal hospital at El-Taef. I saw him with pyjamas between his hands. When I sat on the edge of the bed he gave me the pyjamas and asked:

---

[37] Maḥmūd Shuqayr, *Ṭuqūs*..., p. 20.

– Friend, are you Egyptian?

I answered with most sad tunes:

– No. I am Tunisian.

He was confused. And I heard him saying: Tunisian, more than one time, as one remembered something, he shouted:

– North of Africa.

I smiled in silence. I was overwhelmed again with sad feelings, with illness, and alienation. My tears trickled on my cheeks, and then I wept.

When I opened my eyes I saw him sitting on the opposite bed. He was wiping his tears with his hands…

But I did not figure out was he weeping for my alienation, or for his…[38]

Several conclusions can be drawn upon studying the presented texts, perhaps the most important of which is that the experiences of writing microfiction stories have reached a great deal in modern Arabic literature, which confirms that they represent a distinct literary and creative value. The intensification adopted in those texts, and the use of innovative methods in employing the language, and making it a servant to the brief narrative process, as well as approaching the thresholds of poetry, and taking from it, quoting and intertextualizing, indicates the specificity of this literary genre, and the skill of the authors in dealing with it. One of the characteristic of the studied texts is that they are of varying length, but they all remain in the category of the very short story, never exceeding it. This, of course, is consistent with the characteristics of this art, which is written with the effect of a splash of instantaneous feeling, which tends to generate a pleasant shock in the mind of the recipient. The conclusions drawn from the analysis of the stories studied demonstrate that its very short form has no effect on the diversity of its subjects. It can be said that the themes of these texts are very diverse, touching the environments of the heroes and depicting realistic aspects of their lives. The microfiction authors are also interested in highlighting the common human apprehension and overall human suffering, which makes their works take on a global characteristic despite their local features. From this standpoint, it can be strongly argued that the progress of the modern Arabic narrative has increased with the development of the very short story, whose strong presence in Arabic literature can no longer be denied.

[38] Ibrāhīm Darġūthī, *Under…*, p. 52.

References

Darġūthī, Ibrāhīm, *Under Warm Sun*, in: *Taḥta samā' dāfi'a*, trans. H. Hegazy, Ad-Dār ath-Thaqāfiyya li-n-nashr wa at-tawzī', Tunis 2014.

Dāya, Muḥammad Ruḍwān ad-, *Abū al-Baqā' ar-Rundī Shā'ir al-Andalus*, 'Ālam al-Kutub li-ṭ-Ṭibā'a wa an-nashr wa at-tawzī', Beirut 1986.

Ḥammūdī, Bāsim 'Abd al-Ḥamīd, *Riḥla ma'a al-qiṣṣa al-'irāqiyya*, Dār ar-Rashīd li-n--nashr, Baghdad 1980.

Hemingway E., *In Our Time: The 1924 Text*, University of Victoria, Canada 2015.

Ḥijjū, Muḥammad, *Rubbamā sawfa qad yakūnu*, Al-Ha'ya al-Miṣriyya al-'Āmma li-l--Kitāb, Cairo 2017.

Ḥusayn, Aḥmad Jāsim al-, *Al-qiṣṣa al-qaṣīra as-sūriyya wa naqduhā fī al-qarn al-'ishrīn*, Ittihād al-Kuttāb al-'Arab, Damascus 2001.

Ḥusayn, Aḥmad Jāsim al-, *Al-qiṣṣa al-qaṣīra jiddan... Muqāraba taḥlīliyya*, Dār at-Takwīn li-n-nashr, Damascus 2010.

Ibn Manẓūr, Muḥmmad ibn Mukarram, *Lisān al-'Arab*, Vol. 3, Dār Ṣādir, Beirut 1994.

Leś M.M., *Flash fiction. Krótko o najkrótszych opowieściach*, in: D. Kulesza (ed.), *Tradycja i przyszłość genologii*, Wydawnictwo Uniwersytetu w Białymstoku, Białystok 2013.

Monroe J.T., *Hispano-Arabic Poetry – a Student Anthology*, University of California Press, Berkeley–Los Angeles–London 1974.

Nājī, Ibrāhīm, *Al-A'māl al-Kāmila*, 3rd ed., Dār ash-Shurūq, Cairo 1996.

Qabbānī, Nizār, *Qaṣā'id mutawaḥḥisha*, Manshūrāt Nizār Qabbānī, Beirut 1970.

The Quran, trans. Talal Itani, ClearQuran, Dallas–Beirut 2012.

Scholes R., *Decoding Papa: 'A Very Short Story' as Work and Text*, in: J.J. Benson (ed.), *New Critical Approaches to the Short Stories of Ernest Hemingway*, Duke University Press, Durham–London 1990.

Shārūnī, Yūsuf ash-, *Dirāsāt fī al-qiṣṣa al-qaṣīra*, Dār Ṭalās li-d-dirāsāt wa an-nashr wa at-tarjama, Damascus 1989.

Shuqayr, Maḥmūd, *Ṭuqūs li-l-mar'a ash-shaqiyya*, Dār ibn Rushd, Amman 1986.

Sustana C., *Flash Fiction Definition and History*, https://www.thoughtco.com/what-is-flash-fiction-2990523 (29.03.2020).

SEBASTIAN GADOMSKI

In the maze of discourses – monodrama *Bāy bāy Ǧīllū* (*Bye Bye Gillo*) by Ṭaha ʻAdnān

In 2013, the theatre group al-Ḥāra from Bayt Ǧalā in Palestine staged the play *Bāy bāy Ǧīllū* by Ṭaha ʻAdnān, a Moroccan writer living in Belgium. The performance directed by Baššār Marquṣ was very well received not only in Palestine, but also in other Arab countries and in Europe. The performance was staged in France, Belgium, Italy and other countries. Naǧlā Qumūʻ from the Tunisian newspaper *aṣ-Ṣabāḥ* wrote that "*Bye Bye Gillo* raises essential humanistic issues in an extremely expressive way".[1] In contrast, Ségolène Thos-Collignon from the French newspaper "La Liberté" described the performance as "ingenious and moving".[2] Ṭaha ʻAdnān's play also drew the attention of the Moroccan director Ibrāhīm al-Hināʼī, who staged it in Marrakech in 2014. Monodrama *Bye Bye Gillo* has not ceased to attract the attention of European directors for almost a decade. In 2012 it was chosen by the Contemporary Drama Forum at the Greek International Theatre Institute, translated into Greek and presented on stage during the Third Meetings of the Contemporary Theatre in Athens. In 2014, the Belgian playwright and director Michael de Cock in collaboration with the Arsenaal Theatre and Moussem Nomadic Play

---

1 Naǧlā Qumūʻ, *Masraḥiyya Bāy bāy Ǧīllū*, http://theaterarts.yoo7.com/t778-topic (14.12. 2019).

2 S. Thos-Collignon, *Bye Bye Gillo*, https://www.frequence-sud.fr/art-19404-bye_bye_gillo_toulon.html (14.12.2019).

Centre staged Ṭaha 'Adnān's monodrama in Brussels. Two years later *Bāy bāy Ğīllū* appeared on the Italian theatre stage. The performance, in collaboration with La Campagnia Italiana di Prosa-Genova was directed by Elena Siri. *Bāy bāy Ğīllū* could be seen in the fall of 2019 at the Tor Bella Monaca Theatre in Rome.

It is worth mentioning that the monodrama written by the Moroccan writer in 2011 won the second prize during the International Monodrama Festival in Fujairah in the United Arab Emirates. A year later it was published for the first time in the collection of *Al-'Āzifa. 'Ašar masraḥiyyāt mūnūdrāmā 'arabiyya* (The Player. Ten Arabic Monodramas) in Fujairah. In the same year, its English translation appeared in the collection titled *Ten Arabic Plays: the Winnings Plays of the International Monodrama Competition, 2012–2014*. Shortly afterwards, the play along with the other two dramas – *Pronto Gaga* by Niḍāl Quwayqa and *Hallo veut dire bonjour* by Ṭarīq Bāša was chosen by the project Dramaturgie Arabe Contemporaine launched as a part of play of the theatre festival in Avignon.

The aim of this French cultural project was above all to promote Arabic drama outside the borders of the Arab world. The partners of this undertaking were the Palestinian group al-Ḥāra, the Tunisian al-Tiyātrū (El Teatro) and SHAMS – The Cooperative Cultural Association for Youth in Theatre and Cinema from Lebanon.[3] Soon, the monodrama directed by the aforementioned Baššār Marquṣ and staged by the al-Ḥāra group became a part of play of the official program of events within the project of Marseille-Provence, European Capital of Culture 2013. The same year the next edition of Ṭaha 'Adnān's monodrama was published in bilingual French and Arabic version.

From the very beginning the monodrama *Bāy bāy Ğīllū* was closely connected with the private experiences of its author Ṭaha 'Adnān. This Moroccan writer from Safi has been living permanently in Brussels since 1996, where he currently works for Faderation Wallonie-Bruxelles. In 2003 the first volume of his poems *Wa-lī fihā 'anākib uḫrà* (Transparencies) was published. In 2006 the same collection was published in French under the title *Transparances*. Three years later, the poet published another poetry collection entitled *Akrah al-ḥubb* (I Hate Love). Its French and Spanish translation was published in 2010. In 2012, in Belgium Ṭaha 'Adnān's short story titled *Marokkaans alsjeblieft* (Moroccan Please) was

[3] Cf. http://www.enpicbcmed.eu/communication/dramaturgie-arabe-contemporaine-project-avignon-festival (10.06.2020).

published. Two years ago his second monogram, *Dunya*, was published in Belgium. During his stay in his homeland, the Moroccan writer was very much involved in the promotion of literature and, above all, poetry. In 1990 in Marrakech, together with his brother, he founded a magazine "L'Algarade" devoted to the poetry. In Brussels, he has been managing the salon of Arabic literature for several years and has coordinated the evenings of Arabic romantic poetry in Belgium.[4]

Bāy bāy Ğīllū monodrama which has gained such great recognition from critics and spectators themselves during countless performances in the Middle East and in Europe, tells the story of al-Ğīlālī, a young Moroccan who, despite his own will, became an immigrant and stays illegally in Brussels. We meet him on the day of his extradition from Belgium. Accompanied by two policemen, he embarks on a plane to take him to Morocco. He shakes with fear, afraid of the first flight in his life. The strong shock he experiences when being in a cramped and closed place and the feeling of horror that causes in him boarding the plane make him remember his childhood, when he dreamed of becoming a pilot and soaring through the sky, like birds. He remembers school games when he sang with other children a cheerful song *Fly, fly a pigeon* and imitated the flight of an unrivalled bird. This play absorbed him so much that the teacher had to force him to "land again". Then, in his memories, he returns to his family home in Morocco, difficult relationships with his father and his mother's severity. Finally, he also recollects his immigration life.

We are gradually discovering the biography of al-Ğīlālī, who from the very birth lived in the shadow of rejection, contempt, defeat and constant struggle with adversity. After the death of his father, when the boy was just before the high school diploma, his mother offered him a trip to Europe. She took advantage of the opportunity that came with her husband's funeral. When her brother-in-law arrived from Belgium for the ceremony she persuaded him to take his nephew with him. Al-Ğīlālī did not have much to say. He felt strange. He had the impression that he was no longer welcome at home. He was not convinced by his mother's argument that she had two of his siblings to bring up and pay for their education. He says: "You could say she wanted to get rid of me. Whatever the outcome, a trip to Belgium, a country of chocolate, cheese and blondes, suited me a lot".[5] So, in a rather specific atmosphere and with mixed feelings he left his school,

---

[4] Cf. https://www.etonnants-voyageurs.com/spip.php?article17659 (10.06.2020).

[5] Ṭaha ʻAdnān, *Bāy bāy Ğīllū*, Tunis 2013, p. 16.

friends and family. Obedient to his mother and uncle he hid under the back seat of a car of his relatives and illegally crossed the Moroccan border. Hidden in an extremely uncomfortable place, he almost suffocated and experienced a claustrophobic attack, but thanks to his uncle's bribe he managed to deceive customs officers and eventually found himself in Europe.

It didn't take long before al-Ǧīlālī realized that his life in Belgium and staying with his relatives differed from his ideas and expectations. At his uncle's home no one respected him and everyone treated him like a servant or cheap labour force. The two cousins he looked after during their stay in Morocco now made fun of him and mocked their "bledard" (homeland cousin) at every opportunity. In this situation, al-Ǧīlālī rebelled. He ran away from relatives. First, he wandered around Brussels. He escaped from the police and pimps. He was exposed to countless dangers, but as he says: "I have learned to be distrustful. . . . I survived those days as if I was at war or in a ceasefire waiting for the final solution".[6] Then he decided to go to Denmark, as he recalls, "to check if the grass there really is as green as they say".[7] To survive he stole and claimed to be a refugee from Iraq who is seeking asylum and trying to legalize his stay in Europe. He was soon detained by the police and ordered to leave Denmark. Al-Ǧīlālī also decided to give up his real name and began to use his old nickname Gillo, which his schoolmates had given him during his school days.

> Gillo is a name that is easy to pronounce . . . well sounding, which means nothing. With this name you can start a polite, democratic conversation with the whole world. When someone asked me about my origin, I thought up the appropriate citizenship depending on the origin and position of the questioner.[8]

After returning to Brussels, he found a shared flat with colleagues who, like him, tried to survive somehow and often had problems with the law. Gillo had a Belgian girl for some time. He said about her: "Lisabeth . . . is the most beautiful thing that happened to me in this country".[9] However, they broke up after a short period of time. Lisabeth did not want to be with a boyfriend who was staying in her country illegally and had problems

---

6 Ibid., p. 38.
7 Ibid.
8 Ibid., p. 11.
9 Ibid., p. 21.

with the law. Finally, Gillo was detained by the Belgian police. After a short investigation and a quick trial, he was deported to Morocco. In the last scene of the drama Gillo gets a panic attack on the board of the plane. Like a bird locked in a cage, he tries to break free from the place of his imprisonment. Two cops try to calm him down and choke him with a passenger pillow. Gillo, unable to catch his breath, suffocates and falls dead.

Undoubtedly, Ṭaha ʻAdnān's play breaks the picture of a perfect Western Europe full of mutual respect, understanding and equal opportunities for everyone. *Bāy bāy Ǧīllū* also deconstructs the stereotypical image of an Arab immigrant a smart opportunist who makes cold calculations about his profit and loss balance. Above all, however, the monodrama of the Moroccan writer attacks the cognitive models that dominate our social relations based on which we classify and assess an individual thus losing his subjectivity and individuality. Ṭaha ʻAdnān's play exposes stereotypes, but also shows various types of narratives and discourses that prevail over our thinking, value systems and cognitive tools. It is the discourse or the discourses in *Bāy bāy Ǧīllū*, that are especially clearly present.

Research conducted by Michel Foucault, Jacques Derrida, Teun van Dijk, Norman Fairclough and many other scholars of different disciplines indicate that we are currently experiencing a real flood of discourses in our everyday lives. Staying in social relations, we are their senders and recipients. According to Šammā Bin Muḥammad Bin Ḫālin Āl Nahyān, discourses differ in form, content and type. They are local, regional and global. They can be closely related to a specific historical period, but they often go beyond the rigid temporal framework. Discourses are transmitted through various means. We find them in oral statements, written texts, verbal and non-verbal signs. The sender of the discourse or its exponent can be both the individual and the whole community. Discourses are complex and carry with them many linguistic, cultural, social or political dimensions. The Arab researcher claims that in order to fully understand the social relationships we are part of, we need to understand the great role that discourses play in them.[10]

First of all we should ask the question what discourse is? What does this commonly used term actually mean?

The beginnings of the popularity of this term are associated with linguistics. Initially, the term discourse was associated with ways of describing the

---

10 Cf. Šammā Bin Muḥammad Bin Ḫālin Āl Nahyān, *Taḥlīl al-ḫiṭāb... fahm aḏ-ḏāt wa-al-aḫar*, https://www.alittihad.ae/wejhatarticle/71703/ (15.10.2019).

degree of language organization in a statement. Paul Ricoeur claims that Plato and Aristotle already recognized this concept and carried out their analysis considering language as a discourse.[11] Zellig S. Harris, a transformational grammar propagator, used the term discourse analysis as the formal analysis of the structure of continuous text.[12] The study of complex speech acts and written texts in relation to their social contexts began also to be referred to as discourse analysis.[13] Mikhail Bachtin also drew attention to the issue of linking the statement and its meaning with social practice. In his research, language as a way of speaking was not neutral. He expressed a specific social practice that gave words specific meanings and connotations. Therefore, it was the social community that gave words and all statements meaning.

A similar perspective of language analysis is brought by critical linguistics, which more than sociolinguistics tried to include the issues of power and social hierarchy more than sociolinguistics. In the approaches of its representatives, such as Norman Fairclough, discourse becomes a category connecting texts with participants of the communication. Fairclough himself in his discourse analysis pointed out how language and meaning are used by the authorities.[14]

Over time, discourse as a concept with a fairly wide semantic field was also taken over by sociology and social sciences. Its understanding was soon influenced by the theoretical assumptions of particular fields of knowledge that used it. As David Howarth writes, positivists and proponents of empiricism argue that discourses are best treated as cognitive frameworks or schemas.[15] Thus, discourses as a cognitive framework serve to "intentionally shape commonly shared ideas and meanings in accordance with specific goals".[16] Realistic concepts of discourse, as David Howarth explains, pay more attention to "ontological aspects of discourse theory and analysis".[17] The starting point is the belief that the social world consists of a set of objects that have their own properties and are subject to a certain order.

---

[11] Cf. P. Ricoeur, *Język, tekst, interpretacja*, trans. P. Graff, K. Rosner, PIW, Warszawa 1989, pp. 65–66.

[12] Cf. https://www.britannica.com/science/linguistics/Semantics#ref35093 (15.06.2020).

[13] Cf. A. Duszak, N. Faiclough (eds.) *Krytyczna analiza dyskursu. Interdyscyplinarne podejście do komunikacji społecznej*, Universitas, Kraków 2008, p. 9.

[14] Cf. D. Howarth, *Dyskurs*, trans. A. Gąsior-Niemiec, Oficyna Naukowa, Warszawa 2005, p. 17.

[15] Cf. ibid., pp. 14–15.

[16] Cf. ibid., p. 15.

[17] Cf. ibid.

Thus, discourses are also specific objects and are closely related to other social objects such as the state or economic processes.[18] Representatives of this approach pay a lot of attention to language and texts that are closely related to the spaces in which they arise. Therefore, it is the material world that produces discourses. The analysis of discourses is a question about the impact of this world on social reality.

Connections of discourses with the material world are used by thinkers influenced by Marxism. In their view, discourse analysis reveals mechanisms of hiding economic and social inequalities. Thus, discourse is an ideological system of meanings produced by privileged factors.[19] The next step in the evolution of the concept of discourse was the research conducted by the already mentioned Norman Fairclough, which resulted in a critical analysis of discourse combining many sociological and philosophical concepts. On the structural theory of Anthony Giddens, it was emphasized that discourse as a carrier of meaning and understanding plays a fundamental role in explaining the social world. As Howarth writes, the purpose of discourse analysis was to reveal the mechanisms by which language and meaning are used by power.[20]

The discourse finally found its place in much more general concepts, whose representatives such as Ernesto Laclau and Chantal Mouffe studied the political and historical conditions of its functioning. Discourse and socio-political reality in which it arises and operates have become a particularly important field of study and analysis in recent decades.

According to Michel Foucault, discourse does not arise in a vacuum, but is born and shaped in society. It is influenced by political, cultural and many other factors. The discourse expresses a certain knowledge system of the society, its values and ambitions. It combines in its structure and concretizes knowledge and power. In addition, discourse not only describes reality, but also co-shapes it. Foucault in his reflections on discourse particularly emphasizes the importance of power. He wrote: "Discourse is not only something that explains struggles and reign systems, but it is also something because of what and why we fight – it is the power we are trying to rich".[21] Michael Fleischer, supplementing the reflection on the role of the community that creates the discourse, writes:

---

18 Cf. ibid., p. 16.

19 Cf. ibid.

20 Cf. ibid., p. 17.

21 M. Foucault, *Porządek dyskursu. Wykład inauguracyjny wygłoszony w College de France 2 grudnia 1970*, trans. M. Kozłowski, słowo/obraz terytoria, Gdańsk 1998, p. 8.

> Discourse is a culturally determined way of how and by which interpreters a given subculture communicates, expresses itself in the world of signes, it means in culture, and ensures its coherence. Thus the discourse creates the cultural reality of a given formation which generates it from existing or new material. It causes and ensures its discretion, and thus creates it and is created by it. There is the power of the language system and the power of discourse. Discourses are a kind of "necessary and binding habits of expression".[22]

The goal of discourse theory, as David Howarth writes, is "to discover historically conditioned rules and conventions responsible for producing meanings in specific contexts".[23]

Therefore, discourse as the basic way of expressing the individual and his perceptions about himself and another in the context of culture and the environment to which he belongs forces us to interpretation. The discourse carries a specific message that the sender directs towards the recipient. This message tells us about the sender, but also has a specific impact on the recipient. Finally, the content of this message must be read, analysed, and interpreted. This task is not easy, especially because, as I mentioned, discourses are complex and require a versatile approach. Therefore, in the analysis of discourses, we need a strategy that will enable us to read properly and interpret the messages that they contain.

Teun van Dijk believes that discourse analysis "has become not only a wide-ranging and interdisciplinary undertaking, involving at least several disciplines, but also a sophisticated instrument that can be used in many fields".[24] Currently, discourse analysis as a strategy for reading combines a number of different specialties such as linguistics, literary studies, cultural studies, psychology, sociology, philosophy, and other specializations. Therefore, it is difficult to talk about any one coherent methodology because discourse analysis uses different methodologies in an attempt to capture discourses of a complex and heterogeneous nature. Šammā Bin Muḥammad Bin Ḫālin Āl Nahyān claims that the most common strategy of discourse analysis is currently its linguistic analysis.[25] In this perspective, discourse is treated as a language unit and as such consists of a series

---

22 M. Fleischer, *Konstrukcja rzeczywistości*, Oficyna Wydawnicza Atut, Wrocław 2002, p. 42.

23 D. Howarth, *Dyskurs*, p. 197.

24 T. van Dijk (ed.), *Dyskurs jako struktura i proces*, trans. G. Grochowski, Wydawnictwo Naukowe PWN, Warszawa 2001, p. 47.

25 Cf. Šammā Bin Muḥammad Bin Ḫālin Āl Nahyān, *Taḥlīl al-ḫiṭāb*...

of sentences and statements that make up texts or discourses. Thus, discourse analysis means an analysis of the language used in it, paying attention to its content and structure. The sender's use of language, either oral or written, to convey specific content to the addressee is also important. In the opinion of the Arab researcher, such a strategy helps us learn the language rules governing the structure of discourse. Discourse, as Šammā Bin Muḥammad Bin Ḫālin Āl Nahyān continues, is inscribed in linguistic processes and in principle can only be understood through language. The latter is closely related to the socio-cultural space in which it operates. Therefore, a sociological and cultural perspective must be included in the strategy of discourse analysis.[26] According to this approach, every theory of discourse and theory of its analysis must necessarily contain a theory concerning society.

The discourse being a sort linguistic structure reflects the mutual relations of its users. It discovers a space of knowledge that shapes the consciousness of individuals about the social world around them. On the other hand, it is society that defines how individuals use language. These methods, however, are various and differ depending on the cultural or cognitive background. This creates a large number of discourses that can be detected in society.[27] The discourse reveals the nature of relationships between members of a given community and reveals its structure. In addition, according to Šammā Bin Muḥammad Bin Ḫālin Āl Nahyān, the discourse reveals the nature of the dominant culture in society. It says a lot about its values, the system of producing meanings and methods of exchanging information among individuals.[28] Therefore, discourse analysis allows us to study models of dominant narratives in society. Thanks to it, we can learn the relationships that connect discourses with institutions of power – institutions creating and interpreting meanings. Discourse analysis shows the flow channels of certain narratives and methods of their transmission. In this way, it becomes a tool for better understanding the position of the individual in society.

In the opinion of the aforementioned Teun van Dijk, the analysis of discourse should never stop solely on the linguistic structures themselves and be limited to a linguistic perspective. According to the Dutch scholar "We should look beyond discourse taking into account its cognitive, social,

26 Ibid.
27 Ibid.
28 Ibid.

cultural and historical environments".[29] In his opinion, discourse has three dimensions: the use of language, saturation of discourse with some idea and social interactions that arise in its context.[30] So what Teun van Dijk draws particular attention to is the context of discourse formation.

In order to properly examine this context, the field of research should be significantly expanded to include a number of aspects. Since discourse expresses various content using various means, its analysis methods should be based on various methodologies and experience of different specializations, as indicated by Norman Fairclough. Critical discourse analysis, as I mentioned before, combines many fields of science and becomes a helpful method of reflection on discourse in many areas of our lives. Literary studies can be here a good example. Discourse analysis as part of literary studies, enabled a significant expansion of the context of studies and analysis. Currently, as Michał Markowski and Anna Burzyńska write,

> We avoid creating rules or seeking justifications for the methods of interpreting literary works, but rather expand the scope of literary studies with new cultural contexts. Thanks to this, it seems that reading literary texts has become more creative.[31]

In addition to multidimensional interpretations, the criticism of discourse adds a pragmatic view to literary studies.

It should be noted that Michel Foucault, for example, in his discourse analysis did not examine literary texts. He focused on scientific discourses. Despite this, his theories and the ideas of other scholars who dealt with discourse became an impulse and a starting point for new literary studies. The literary text consciously or not constitutes a carrier of discourses and its content reflects social processes and activities. The writer does not follow only his inspiration, which takes him into some isolated, neutral and entirely imagined world. Above all, he lives in a society that creates, duplicates and transmits various discourses. Therefore, the presence of discourses in literary texts as cultural texts is something natural. Similarly, the

---

[29] T. van Dijk, *Kontekstualizacja w dyskursie parlamentarnym. Aznar, Irak i pragmatyka kłamania*, in: A. Duszak, N. Faiclough (eds.), *Krytyczna analiza dyskursu, Interdyscyplinarne podejście do komunikacji społecznej*, trans. J. Piotrowski, p. 216.

[30] Cf. A. Synowiec, *W stronę analizy tekstu – wprowadzenie do teorii dyskursu*, "Zeszyty Naukowe Politechniki Śląskiej" 2013, z. 65, p. 393.

[31] A. Burzyńska, M.P. Markowski, *Teorie literatury XX wieku. Podręcznik*, SIW Znak, Kraków 2006, p. 40.

reader or recipient of a literary production is not just a seeker and tracker of the meanings that the author left for him. The reader also in his natural, social position is an exponent of discourses and their sender. His sense of aesthetics, value system, beliefs about the world in which he lives and his position in society are largely shaped by a number of discourses. In a sense he is the result of discourses in which it is sunk. What's more, his cognitive tools and the entire epistemological system are also based on models recorded and reproduced by discourses.

Undoubtedly, the assumptions of discourse analysis have contributed to the emergence of new specializations such as, for example, new historicism, cultural criticism. From their part, they significantly influenced literary studies. New historicism as a school of literary criticism draws attention to the importance of the historical context in the process of reading and interpreting a literary work. This school treats the text primarily as a product of a specific time, environment or external circumstances. To the background pushes the original and independent creativity of its author. Reading a literary text and its interpretation constitute a continuous process of determining the ideological, social and political position of the reader in a particular cultural environment.

Cultural criticism defines literature as a product of practicing discourses. They define it and govern its social foundations. An author and a reader are subject to specific ideologies that dominate at a certain time. It is according to these ideologies that they both play their own social roles. The meaning of a literary work arises as a result of social practice.[32]

These theories confirm the importance of discourse analysis in the humanities and affirm its importance in literary studies.

As I mentioned earlier, language is the basic material subject to research in the complex and many-sided process of discourse analysis. As Teun van Dijk writes, its task is:

> to provide an integrated description of the three dimensions of communication: how a given use of language affects a person's image of the world, the course of interaction, and vice versa how various aspects of interaction determine the form of expression, as well as how the beliefs held by participants communication determines the choice of specific language means.[33]

---

[32] Cf. ibid., p. 539.

[33] T. van Dijk, *Badania nad dyskursem*, in: T. van Dijk (ed.), *Dyskurs jako struktura*..., p. 10.

The language of a literary text largely reflects the situation of a given language in everyday life. The author's linguistic imagination and sensitivity obviously go beyond the everyday use of language, but it is this colloquiality in all its richness and complexity that is the natural point of reference for the writer. The language of a literary work is not born in a neutral environment, but reflects the social and ideological environment close to its author. The language of a literary work finally carries and expresses discourses. On the one hand, these discourses fill the space that shapes the author's personality and his perception of the world in the social, political, ideological dimension, etc. On the other, they fill the space of a literary text. They become an integral part of the setting – the broadly understood ideological background of a literary work. Protagonists express various discourses in direct or indirect way. Often, conflicts between the characters are the result of a collision of different, contradictory attitudes, beliefs, but also discourses they represent and express.

The monodrama *Bāy bāy Ğīllū*, which is both a literary and a cultural text, carries many discourses that shape its ideological context and in a sense determine the position of its main character. Michel Foucault emphasized the heterogeneous nature of discourses and what draws our attention in the monodrama by Ṭaha ʻAdnān is the fact that Gillo as one character is the exponent of many different discourses. Various ideologies and interests are mixed up in them, which creates sometimes quite an inconsistent or even contradictory picture of the hero. He not only lives in a network of discourses without being fully aware of that, but also through his language and behaviour expresses them and convey them to others. It is not without reason that the mentioned Palestinian director Baššāra Marquṣ decided that the role of the hero was performed by three actors. Each of them presented a specific stage in Gillo's life: in Morocco, in exile and on board the aircraft that was to take him to his homeland. Each stage reflects the specific life situation of the hero and his emotional and mental state. In addition to that, through Gillo's statements and behaviour each stage also brings a large load of discourses. Their traces are hidden above all in his words, but also in his attitude. This multitude of "characters" accumulated in one hero emphasizes the unique situation in which he finds himself and corresponds to the multitude of discourses that create his image of the world and determine his place.

Discourses and their traces, which we find in the monodrama *Bāy bāy Ğīllū*, carry a lot of stereotypes and common social imaginations, which become a starting point and an excuse to raise certain topics. What Gillo experiences in specific circumstances becomes a reason to express his truth about the world, his life and others. Discourses in the play take the form of socially transmitted and sanctioned ideological, political and cultural beliefs. These become the driving force for undertaking certain actions. They are the implementation of so-called worldviews, established opinions and common beliefs that reduce an individual and his experience to statements and judgements of a general nature.

As I mentioned, Ṭaha 'Adnān's monodrama is full of discourses, and their traces can be found at every stage of the play's development. However, the most dominant are the broadly understood discourse of power, a discourse on immigration and a discourse on the West. At the same time, we must remember that they all intertwine with each other and with other discourses, and it is very difficult to abstract them from the complex cognitive structure and a body of knowledge that is expressed by the hero of the play.

Gillo's problems, as he says, began as a consequence of his father's decision to name him after his friend – al-Ğīlālī. This name that the hero of the play considers bizarre and tiring has become a lifelong burden for him. He says:

> You certainly know this hadith which encourages the faithful to give their children the names of the prophets; but the fact that it inspires them to give their children names after friends is a real heresy! What did I do to you, father, that you dressed gave me such an old-fashioned name that I have to carry with me like a crutch my whole life like a crutch![34]

Of course, we can ask the question about the reason for such strong aversion, and even hatred of the name? Gillo gives us the answer. He says: "For example, in shows I watched on TV, do you think I've ever come across an engineer, doctor or even a nurse? No, al-Ğīlālī is always some naive peasant, some stupid janitor, or a pathetic vegetable seller".[35] Because of his name, even at school, his life was not easy. Gillo adds: "When you bear this type of name, you quickly realize that your classmates are really bastards and they will not miss any opportunity to poison your life: they will make you curse even the day you were born with such a stupid name".[36] Gillo also explains

[34] Ṭaha 'Adnān, *Bāy bāy Ğīllū*, p. 10.
[35] Ibid., p. 11.
[36] Ibid.

the reason for his disgust for his own name. He says: "What bothers me the most is the fact that every time I am forced to pronounce it: al . . . Ǧī . . . lā . . . lī. The name that begins with 'al' clearly sounds Arabic. Such a name suggests identity with all the complications that come with it".[37] He also adds:

> If one day I have a child, I will give him a name that is not associated with anything at all. In this uncertain world this will be one certain thing for him. For a poor boy born in this country it is not good to have a strange name. Because although it would be the most innocent, one day it may prove to be the prime prosecution evidence. They stop you and after a few days of interrogation let you free because they eventually realize that they were wrong, that your name strangely reminded them of the alleged terrorist. In this way, you are doomed to the risk that you will lead your life tossing from one suspicion to another.[38]

So after such confessions, if we said that the hero of the play suffered from identity problems, that he had low self-esteem and that for one reason or another he didn't feel proud of his nationality or ethnicity, we certainly would not be mistaken. However, we would not be mistaken if we also said that Gillo as a human was a victim of stereotypes, so-called social practice, the domination of a certain way of thinking that shaped social attitudes and common beliefs. It turns out that the completely innocent decision of the father regarding the name he will give his son can bring unexpected, but very far-reaching consequences. Al-Ǧīlālī does not find enough strength to face direct and open hostility towards his person for a trivial and unimportant reason. Somehow in response to the peculiar stigmatization he had experienced in his childhood, he decided to replace his real name with a nickname his colleagues had given him. "Gillo" became an escape from everything that it carried in itself and what was al-Ǧīlālī. His nickname is a shelter from others and in fact, from himself as well. However, Gillo quickly realizes that he cannot escape from the world that surrounds him and from himself. This is particularly clear in Europe. At one point, the hero of the monodrama dreams about only one thing. He would like to be able to become invisible. He says:

> If only I had a magic hat that would make me invisible, I would use it immediately. . . . I appear and disappear. I disappear to overcome this incomplete

---

[37] Ibid., p. 12.
[38] Ibid., p. 13.

> presence. I turn away from the world that is afraid of my existence. I run away from people and their inquiring looks, which force me to ask for forgiveness. I run away from their chronic suspicion towards me, me who is as harmless as an innocent lie.[39]

Then he adds:

> Of course, you've never experienced the feeling of being an unwanted person! Persona non grata. I live with it every day and if I feel like disappearing, it is because I want to see the world more clearly. So I don't have to turn my head like an offended maid when you look at me. I want to disappear to keep the picture of the world for longer. Hiding is a million times better than experiencing such a curse in daylight.[40]

Gillo wants to free himself from a world that accurately determines his place and qualifies him according to measures and standards that he does not understand nor accept. The hero of the play wants to get out of the "social cage" in which he found himself against his will. Of course, his dream of neutrality, full independence and freedom in the space of social relations remains only in the sphere of unfulfilled dreams and utopian ideas. The character of Gillo reminds us of the hero of the famous novel *Invisible Man* by Ralph Ellison. The nameless main character of the American novel says:

> I am an invisible man. No, I am not a spook like those who haunted Edgar Allan Poe; nor am I one of your Hollywood-movie ectoplasms. I am a man of substance, of flesh and bone, fiber and liquids – and I might even be said to possess a mind. I am invisible, understand, simply because people refuse to see me. Like the bodiless heads you see sometimes in circus sideshows, it is as though I have been surrounded by mirrors of hard, distorting glass. When they approach me they see only my surroundings, themselves, or figments of their imagination – indeed, everything and anything except me.[41]

Then he adds: "Nor is my invisibility exactly a matter of a bio-chemical accident to my epidermis. That invisibility to which I refer occurs because

39 Ibid., p. 34.
40 Ibid., p. 35.
41 Ralph Ellison, *Invisible Man*, Vintage International, New York 1995, p. 3.

of a peculiar disposition of the eyes of those with whom I come in contact. A matter of the construction of their inner eyes, those eyes with which they look through their physical eyes upon reality".[42] The difference, however, is that the invisibility of the hero of Ellison's novel over time becomes an attitude of struggle against racial segregation, prejudice and caste system of American society. For Gillo, invisibility is a form of escape from stereotypes, clichés and socially sanctioned cognitive models.

Teun Van Dijk writes that the subject of discourse analysis is statement and text in context.[43] The pretext for Gillo's highly emotional expressions is the situation he finds himself in. His words are a verbal reaction to how he is perceived and treated. During the police interrogation, he says: "When you feel that you mean nothing, you become capable of everything and ready for anything".[44] Then he adds:

> Didn't your ancestors bother to colonize us? And mine, they chased them out of too much stupidity. But that was just a historical misunderstanding. If I'm here today, it's to explain myself. I came in an act of spontaneous submission asking you to colonize me. Well, Ok. I agree. Integrate me. Change my name. If you don't like Gillo, call me Jacques, Gilbert or Jean-Marie. Call me Marie, it will be shorter. This is not a problem for me. Just make me an identity that can be shown in broad daylight. Don't make me run into the dark. Am I not a human being like you? Is it my fault that I was accidentally born in the wrong place? . . . I can never understand why some treat you like a dog and at the same time blame you for barking and biting![45]

Just as in an act of desperation, Gillo breaks free from escorting police officers, so with his words and what he says he wants to break free from the cage of notions and definitions in which he was locked up as an Arab, an illegal immigrant and a small thief. In an ironic tone, he indicates that he is ready to do anything to be accepted and treated like a human. Others determined his identity. They assigned it to a specific file in a collection of court records and in a specific space of social imaginations. Meanwhile, he doesn't know who he is anymore. Just as he did not choose a name for

[42] Ibid., p. 11.
[43] Cf. Teun van Dijk, *Badania nad dyskursem*, p. 12.
[44] Ṭaha ʻAdnān, *Bāy bāy Ǧīllū*, p. 32.
[45] Ibid., p. 33.

himself, he was not the one who decided to go to Belgium. Although he does not hide that the prospect of going to Brussels suited him very much, he can not get rid of the feeling of rejection he experienced in his family home. He addresses his mother: "You threw me out as if I were a lousy dog. It is because of you that I live like a tramp in this country that gives me only loneliness and anguish. . . . What did I do to you to get rid of me like that?"[46] Chased from his own house, rejected by others, he asks quoting the lyrics of the song that was sang by the Tunisian singer ʻUliyya at-Tūnisiyya: "Who am I? I ask myself. Where is my place in this world? Who am I?"[47]

Gillo gives the impression that he has been incapacitated in a sense. Someone else made the most important decisions in his life instead of him and on his behalf. Someone designated a place to live for him and defined his identity. His father, by giving him the name al-Ğīlālī symbolically pushed Gillo's life in a specific direction, burdening him with a peculiar stigma from his childhood. For his name, also in a symbolic dimension, he was stigmatized from an early age. He experienced rejection from the side of his family and school mates, in his immediate environment. In Belgium, without a residence permit, he was also doomed to rejection or to life on the margins, at best. He says:

> I am an illegal being. Normally I should ask for forgiveness for living, for this absurd existence that I have. For this existence, which in legal terms is equal to non-existence. And even worse because it is a clear violation of the law. I would like to be a refugee from Palestine, Iraq, Chechnya, Somalia or Haiti. . . . Being a victim of a civil war, a natural disaster, or whatever the misfortune, just to gain your sympathy, that my case would be worthy of your attention. . . . I am a grouchy cat sulking at a wedding party. I'm so grotesque.[48]

Of course, Gillo's complaints do not change anything, but they make him more and more aware that he is a toy in the hands of others, that his own decisions basically mean little. His obedience to his mother and uncle, which is to ensure a better future for him, becomes basically the source of his misfortunes. With irony and sarcasm, he recalls uncle's words: "Illegal work will give you legal money that will allow you to get a legal

46 Ibid., p. 46.
47 Ibid., p. 18.
48 Ibid., p. 19.

marriage that might be useful in case of trouble".[49] Then he adds: "Idiot. He had no idea that my biggest troubles had started the day I came to this country with him. He took revenge on me for his two sons, who proved to be complete dumbs".[50]

The widely accepted and reproduced social model, based on which parents decide about the future of their children is shown in the play of the Moroccan writer not only in very direct but even exaggerated way. As a matter of fact Gillo's mother doesn't think so much about her son's future, but takes the opportunity to get rid of him from home. Shortly after leaving Morocco, Gillo learns from his aunt about his mother's morally inappropriate behaviour. Moreover, her financial needs are the main topic of their rare telephone conversations. Gillo works all day at the construction site with his uncle's team to send almost all his money to Morocco. More and more burdens fall on him, with which he can not cope. As it seems, tormented by a sense of moral duty, he is unable to break free from the next cage in which he was caught.

The order of social relations and the so-called social practice carry discourses that we rarely think about. The sense of obedience, respect, the position occupied in family relationships are products of the "natural" social order, universal consent affirmed and reproduced in social practice. This order, whose goal is to ensure the stable development of each community and protect its members does not always fulfil its tasks in the best way. Parental authority, prestige and position do not always guarantee the "proper" start in the life of the young generation. Gillo here is an example – caught up in trouble and sent to misery by his own mother.

Once again it is worth repeating that Gillo is not the originator or initiator of his trip to Belgium. However, his image of Europe is very clear. The myth of the wonderful land where everyone can find a well-paid job and enjoy various means of entertainment is a picture that Gillo has been carrying since childhood. This is of course a stereotype, but also part of a more complex narrative. This is one of the main elements of the discourse about a prosperous, tolerant and open Europe. Undoubtedly, the context of this discourse is primarily material and ideological. These features were emphasized by Teun van Dijk. A rich and free Europe appears here as a contradiction to full of restrictions and poor Morocco. Lack of prospects for the future in Gillo's country is confronted with the vision

---

49 Ibid., p. 37.

50 Ibid.

of adventure and great opportunities in Belgium. This image of Western Europe as a result of some discourse influenced the young man and made him accept a trip to Brussels. However, he quickly learned that this image reproduced by his countrymen is far from the truth and everyday reality. The feeling of disappointment in Europe is also deepened by his unsuccessful relationship with the girl with whom he associated all his hopes. He says:

> Lisabeth, the only stable thing in my unstable life. With her, I came into being through the great door. She brought me books and took me to the cinema. . . . Thanks to her, all the doors were open to me. . . . Lisabeth is my entry card to life with all its cheerfulness.[51]

Like most things in Gillo's life, also his love story was based on a certain illusion, a mirage that ended painfully for him. In a sense, his relationship with Lisabeth was as virtual as the world of the Internet, which he discovered thanks to her. By the way, he discovered also that this parallel world gives him a chance to come into existence somehow. He says: "Thanks to Net I had the impression that I was fully alive. I live and have an address, and even a few addresses and the same number of names that change depending on my interlocutor. I enjoy an excess of identity. . . . I chat so I exist".[52] Of course, such existence is incidental and illusory. It can't replace real identity in the real world. It is hard not to notice the symbolic parallel between this illusory internet identity and the illusory relationship with Lisabeth. We can only guess that for Lisabeth Gillo was just an adventure during which she didn't mind that she was getting stolen gifts from him. However, when she realized that the relationship with an illegal immigrant and a small thief could be dangerous for her, she decided to end it. Over time, Gillo realized that his relationship was really virtual. He says:

> Lisabeth, my shameful truth. The problem is that I loved her so much that I didn't see the sun illuminating the truth. Love and truth are two things that are completely incompatible with each other. To love you need a large dose of illusion. And I find pleasure in this illusion and relish its bitterness.[53]

51 Ibid., pp. 22–24.
52 Ibid., p. 22.
53 Ibid., p. 27.

The myth of a wonderful Europe, the myth of wonderful mutual love with Lisabeth are just illusions for which Gillo must pay. One more time, the main character of the monodrama is once again a victim. Although we could say that his fault is that he cannot critically look at the world around him, that he cannot understand the game in which he participate. To tell the truth about Gillo, it should be said that his way of life in Belgium must sooner or later end with troubles with the police and the law. Besides, he does not claim to be innocent. He says simply: "Yes, I am a thief. . . I confess. But I'm far from being a criminal".[54] Then, in a somewhat grotesque tone, he adds:

> Here on earth it is enough for some bastards to gather cheerfully under a rag, which they will call the banner, and their crimes will soon become heroic. All the heroes in history are really great thieves. The difference is that they steal under the banner of some ideas and everyone treats their thefts as revolutionary acts. I do not defend any idea. I steal without illusion. I steal by necessity. This is my SOS that I send out to draw attention to my existence.[55]

Once again, it should be emphasized that Gillo is not innocent. However, if we take a good look at his life, we will see that his guilt is a consequence of the offenses that others committed against him. In Richard Wright's novel titled *Native Son*, the main character Bigger Thomas commits a crime. The lawyer Boris Max, who defends him in court, is terrified of the decay and corruption of the American society and tries to make the jury realize that socially committed crimes of rejection, marginalization, racism and segregation must give birth to other crimes that members of such society commit against each other. Gillo as an illegal immigrant, Arab, thief meets all the criteria of common stereotypes, clichés and certain labels that stick to a specific group in society. At the same time, Gillo doesn't match fully and unequivocally the abovementioned categorizations. The hero of the Moroccan writer's drama does not fit into the narrow conceptual framework established by social practice. The terms and names that are to define the identities of objects and their nature are insufficient. The reactions provoked by these expressions and descriptions are sometimes inadequate to real situations. Reductions and simplifications that occur when describing objects or phenomena often deprive these objects

[54] Ibid., p. 33.
[55] Ibid.

and phenomena of key features. Reduction and generalization are cognitive and semantic processes that contribute to the structure of discourse. Recalling the theories of Laclau and Mouffe, one could say that the discourse on immigrants that concerns Gillo here is based on the socially exploited system of differences. Gillo's situation, even in his own opinion, is an anomaly, something contradictory to what is perceived as normal and acceptable according to the social consent. With his "abnormality", Gillo in a way weakens the stable system and social order.

Shortly before the court's decision about the future of the Moroccan illegal immigrant, during the interrogation, he asks the policeman: "Treat me like a militant. A militant who fights for the right to a free life in this free prison that you call life".[56] Gillo, on the one hand, mocks a little mockery and on the other refers to rational thinking and such models/cases in which these anomalies are socially accepted. However, Gillo's paradox is that his "exceptional situation" is unprovable. His "special case" cannot be supported by difficult situation in the country, belonging to a persecuted political, ethnic or religious group. Gillo's uniqueness is too common to become a defense and an excuse for him. His ordinariness and abnormalities at the same time mean that his voice means nothing and that he can be silenced in the name of law and general regulations.

Is Gillo really a militant? In a way, yes, because as he says his whole life was a constant struggle with adversities, problems and obstacles. Gillo is a symbolic militant for the case of real human subjectivity in highly conventionalised social relations. His life and situation go beyond the established and acceptable framework. He constitutes also an element of discourses in which he is only an element of a larger structure. Thus, as an individual, he plays the role of an argument, goal and transmitter of various discourses.

In Michael Halliday's opinion, "the text (literary and cultural) is a social occurrence and a semiotic meeting. It mixes the senses and meanings that make up the social system".[57] The play *Bāy bāy Ǧīllū* shows the image of society and the systems that organize it. It is beyond any doubt that discourses play here a fundamental role. It should be emphasized that discourses can play a basic function in creating ideas about reality, modelling ways of

---

56 Ibid., p. 34.

57 M. Halliday, *Text as Semantic Choice in Social Contexts*, in: T. van Dijk, S. Petőfi (eds.), *Grammars and Descriptions: Studies in Text Theory and Text Analysis*, W. de Gruyter, Berlin–New York 1977, p. 197.

thinking and shaping behaviour. At the same time, they can shape cognitive systems and organize knowledge according to specific patterns. Discourses do not remain only in the sphere of cognitive mechanisms, but are manifested in specific decisions and actions of individuals and also entire communities. In this perspective, the discourse analysis of discourses allows us to look critically at social phenomena and mechanisms of which we are part and which constantly affect us. There are many strategies and methodologies for analysing discourses. Each of them, stemming from a specific field of knowledge, emphasizes slightly different aspects. However, they all try to present a coherent description of discourse as one of the basic phenomena in social relations. Literature, for its part, transfers a fragment of reality into a specific space where it can condense a number of phenomena and as if under a microscope, subject them to multilateral examination. Ṭaha ʻAdnān in his drama not only refers to many social phenomena, but also deconstructs them. He shows internal contradictions and cracks in the seemingly coherent system and coherent practices. His attention is focused on a single person who disappears from the field of interest when we reflect upon the complex mechanisms of social relations.

Ṭaha ʻAdnān in his theatre gives voice to those who are too weak to be heard. The Moroccan writer opens a debate on uncomfortable topics. He shows that reality cannot be simplified and reduced to a zero-one model that will ensure peace and harmony in the space of extremely complex social relationships.

References

Burzyńska A., Markowski M.P., *Teorie literatury XX wieku. Podręcznik*, SIW Znak, Kraków 2006.

Dijk T. van (ed.), *Dyskurs jako struktura i proces*, trans. T. Dobrzyńska, Wydawnictwo Naukowe PWN, Warszawa 2001.

Dijk T. van, *Badania nad dyskursem*, in: T. van Dijk (ed.), *Dyskurs jako struktura i proces*, Wydawnictwo Naukowe PWN, Warszawa 2001.

Dijk T. van, *Kontekstualizacja w dyskursie parlamentarnym. Aznar, Irak i pragmatyka kłamania*, in: A. Duszak, N. Faiclough (eds.), *Krytyczna analiza dyskursu. Interdyscyplinarne podejście do komunikacji społecznej*, trans. J. Piotrowski, Universitas, Kraków 2008.

Duszak A., Faiclough N. (eds.), *Krytyczna analiza dyskursu*, Universitas, Kraków 2008.

Ellison R., *Invisible Man*, Vintage International, New York 1995.

Ellison R., *Niewidzialny człowiek*, trans. A. Jankowski, Rebis, Poznań 2004.

Fleischer M., *Konstrukcja rzeczywistości*, Oficyna Wydawnicza Atut, Wrocław 2002.

Foucault M., *Porządek dyskursu. Wykład inauguracyjny wygłoszony w College de France 2 grudnia 1970*, trans. M. Kozłowski, słowo/obraz terytoria, Gdańsk 1998.

Halliday M., *Text as Semantic Choice in Social Contexts*, in: T. van Dijk, S. Petőfi (eds.), *Grammars and Descriptions: Studies in Text Theory and Text Analysis*, W. de Gruyter, Berlin–New York 1977.

Howarth D., *Dyskurs*, trans. A. Gąsior-Niemiec, Oficyna Naukowa, Warszawa 2005.

Nağlā Qumūʻ, *Masraḥiyya Bāy bāy Ğīllū*, http://theaterarts.yoo7.com/t778-topic (14.12.2019).

Ricoeur P., *Język, tekst, interpretacja*, trans. P. Graff, K. Rosner, PIW, Warszawa 1989.

Šammā Bin Muḥammad Bin Ḫālin Āl Nahyān, *Taḥlīl al-ḫiṭāb... fahm aḏ-ḏāt wa-al-aḫar*, https://www.alittihad.ae/wejhatarticle/71703/ (15.10.2019).

Synowiec A., *W stronę analizy tekstu – wprowadzenie do teorii dyskursu*, "Zeszyty Naukowe Politechniki Śląskiej" 2013, z. 65.

Ṭaha ʻAdnān, *Bāy bāy Ğīllū*, Tunis 2013.

Thos-Collignon S., *Bye Bye Gillo*, https://www.frequence-sud.fr/art-19404-bye_bye_gillo_toulon.html (14.12.2019).

http://www.enpicbcmed.eu/communication/dramaturgie-arabe-contemporaine-project-avignon-festival (10.06.2020).

https://www.britannica.com/science/linguistics/Semantics#ref35093 (15.06.2020).

https://www.etonnants-voyageurs.com/spip.php?article17659 (10.06.2020).

اللغة

MARCIN GAJEC

Women in Islamic State propaganda

The Islamic State in Iraq and Syria (Ad-Dawlah al-Islamiyah fi-l-ˁIraq wa-sh-Sham, Daesh) was a terrorist organization that usurped the right to continue the idea of a supranational Muslim empire based on Sharia law – the caliphate. Its core were former military members of the demoralized armed forces of Iraq (later also of Syria) and radical activists of Salafi Jihadist organizations gathered under the black banner of ISIS. As a result of intensive recruitment activities conducted in mosques and religious associations, but also through both traditional and "new" media, thousands of volunteers from Muslim countries and representatives of Muslim minorities from Western Europe, North America and Australia[1] joined ranks of militants. Many of them abandoned their communities, often assimilated with Western culture, and joined the fight on the side of extremists. Almost five thousand women were among them.[2] The Islamic State propaganda, led by a well-organized Al-Hayat media center, played a significant role in encouraging them to make such a heavy decision.

In this work I will focus on two press titles published online in years 2014–2017. Both were professionally published magazines, which distinguishes

1 The United Nations estimates that up to 40,000 volunteers from 110 countries could come to Syria and Iraq and fight on the side of the Islamic State. *Greater Cooperation Needed to Tackle Danger Posed by Returning Foreign Fighters*, https://www.un.org/press/en/2017/sc13097.doc.htm (01.07.2020).

2 These estimates are based on the London International Center for the Study of Radicalisation report of 2018.
J. Cook, G. Vale, *From Daesh to 'Diaspora': Tracing the Women and Minors of Islamic State*, https://icsr.info/wp-content/uploads/2018/07/Women-in-ISIS-report_20180719_web.pdf (01.07.2020), p. 3.

them from numerous amateur network publications. Both also, although to varying degrees were directed to the "Western recipient". Both, finally contained materials directed addressed to women, who until now were not a frequent target for recruitment of international Islamist organizations associated with the world jihad movement.

Dabiq and *Rumiyah*

The first issue of the *Dabiq* magazine was published on July 5, 2014. On June 29, 1435 AH, the month of Ramadan began. On the same day Islamic State announced the creation of a caliphate, headed by Abu Bakr al-Baghdadi as the caliph Ibrahim. The appearance of the first Daesh periodical magazine was not accidental then. At the same time, Al-Hayat Media Center, which is responsible for Islamic State propaganda on the Internet, has intensified its activities. There have been numerous social media entries and videos on YouTube. The number of recipients was growing rapidly, and better quality materials were published. The first attempts to create an e-magazine for a terrorist state were made in the first half of 2014, initially under the name of *Islamic State News*, renamed later to *Islamic State Report*. Positive feedback from readers prompted Al-Hayat to expand this form of contact with potential recruits in Europe (both magazines were published in English).[3]

Dabiq was not the first jihadist journal published on the web. It is often noted that the trail was blazed by *Inspire*, a magazine published by Al-Malahem Media, a web agency representing the Al-Qaeda of the Arabian Peninsula. It was directed to Muslims in the United States and Great Britain who sympathized with Al-Qaeda. From the first issue a specific magazine profile was formed. It published appeals from organization leaders, calls for global jihad, and practical guides on organizing attacks in the Western world.[4] The similarities between the two periodicals are obvious, but there are also some differences. As noted by Harleen K. Gambhir, an analyst at the Washington think tank Institute for the Study of War, *Inspire*

3 "Dabiq", No. 1, p. 3.

4 The first issue, the section "Open Source Jihad" includes the famous and widely commented article titled *Make a bomb in the kitchen of Your Mom*, talking about how to make simple explosives using generally available means: matches, sugar, a piece of pipe, nails, Christmas tree lights and alarm clock. "Inspire", No. 1, pp. 33–40.

was targeted at active jihad fighters, lone wolves who, embedded in Western society, could have made a surprising and tragic attack.[5] The definitely militaristic nature of the magazine limited the group of recipients to a certain group of Al-Qaida supporters who were determined to act. Individual articles, calls and guides were only intended to strengthen readers in the decision already made.

Dabiq was addressed to a wider group of readers. The main edition was prepared in English, but other languages versions; Arabic, German, French, Russian and later Bahasa were also published. 15 issues of the magazine have been published. From the beginning, the magazine was at a fairly high level in terms of editing. Individual articles were illustrated with good quality suggestive photos. ISIS fighters were portrayed as heroes fighting for freedom and truth. Information about the functioning of Daesh and battlefield reports were a regular element. Over time, articles encouraging hijra[6] began to appear. It was emigration to subordinate areas of Daesh that was the main goal that *Dabiq* journalists set for their readers. Unlike *Inspire*, which rather encouraged attacks at the place of residence in the US or Europe.[7] The newspaper grew and became more and more similar to Western magazines. Reports and articles of regular columnists like John Cantlie, and interviews with prominent ISIS activists and commanders made the message more attractive. From the seventh issue new section *To Our Sisters* appeared, which was addressed to women, potential recruits. These particular articles will be the canvas for later analysis.

Dabiq was the main, but not the only magazine in the Al-Hayat Media Center portfolio. It quickly became apparent that translations into other languages were not enough for supporters of organizations not living in English-speaking countries. Thus, publishing of *Dar al-Islam* (in French), *Istok* (in Russian) and *Kostantiniyye* (in Turkish) began. They were addressed more precisely and were intended to reach specific readers. Al-Hayat's goal

---

5 H.K. Gambhir, *Dabiq: The Strategic Messaging of the Islamic State*, http://www.understandingwar.org/sites/default/files/Dabiq%20Backgrounder_Harleen%20Final_0.pdf (13.06.2020).

6 This term, meaning the emigration of the Prophet Muhammad from Mecca to Medina in 622, which marked the beginning of the Islamic era, was used by ISIS ideologists to describe the departure from their native country to the territory of Islamic State. The fighters who decided to take this step were referred to as *muhajirun*. This is an example of appropriating and giving new meanings to the fundamental concepts related to Islam by jihadists. Later in the article, the term hijra will be used in this sense.

7 H.K. Gambhir, *Dabiq...*, pp. 4–5.

was to build the image of Islamic State as a "Muslim paradise", a place where for the first time in centuries it was possible to create a functioning and well-managed state based on Sharia principles. This presentation of Daesh was to support the recruitment of new fighters for the hijra. However, the main recruitment channel were mosques and religious associations dominated by radical Salafi imams and their associates. The online press, like social media, was, however, an important tool to shape the views, especially of young Muslims in Europe.

Various methods of persuasion were used. Salafist scholars, using religious rhetoric, created the belief that traveling to Syria and Iraq and participating in jihad against non-believers is the religious duty of every Muslim.[8] Muslims were portrayed as victims of violence. The perpetrators of attacks and their associates serving their prison sentences in the USA and Europe were described as heroes of fighting in the way of Allah. The policy of Western states towards Muslim minorities was described as persecution. Escape from oppression and the fight for justice in the ranks of ISIS were to be the only solution for a young Muslim in London, Paris, Berlin or Stockholm. The fight itself was presented on the one hand as a difficult duty, but also as an adventure and fulfillment of male fantasies. Suggestive photos showed smiling, bearded fighters triumphing over non-believers. The victorious soldiers not only favored the cause of Islam, but were also awarded temporarily.[9] The importance of brotherhood, friendship and community of believers standing shoulder to shoulder against evil was emphasized. Historical politics was also taken care of and the Islamic interpretation of events and historical figures from the Caliph Abu Bakr as-Siddiq to the 2001 World Trade Center attack was presented in the "From the Pages of History" series.

The name of the magazine refers to one of the hadiths from the Muslim Ibn Hajjaj collection. This is one of the stories attributed to the Prophet Muhammad, the authenticity of which the researchers have no doubt and

---

8 The fundamentalist approach to the term *jihad* as primarily an armed struggle against religious opponents is another example of the appropriation and reinterpretation of Islam's basic concepts. Particularly because, according to the doctrine of the *takfir*, virtually everyone who did not support the Islamic rule of Daesh, including other Sunnis, could be considered an enemy.

9 After capturing Yazidi-dominated Sinjar in northern Iraq in August 2014, thousands of women and children fell into the hands of ISIS soldiers. *Dabiq* journalists, relying on the opinion of specialists in Muslim law, praised the restoration of slavery. Not only loot from the looted city, but also slaves were to be attended by pious fighters of the Islamic State.

unanimously classify him in the category of *sahih.*[10] Abu Hurayra, one of Muhammad's companions, is the transmitter of this tradition, and after the Prophet's death – the teacher and guardian of the Prophet's legacy. The mentioned hadith (Sahih Muslim, Book 54, hadith 44)[11] concerns the fight of Muslims against the Romans, the fall of the false prophet Dajjal and the return of Isa (Jesus) who will lead the believers to victory. The beginning of these events is associated with the clash between the army of Medina (Muslims) and the Christian host of Byzantium (the editors of *Dabiq* consistently identify the Byzantines with the Crusaders, and they reserve this term for their political enemies, i.e. the USA, Western Europe and Russia). This battle is about to take place near Dabiq in Syria, north of Aleppo. After this victory, paid with numerous victims, the believers will conquer Constantinople. In Islamic State rhetoric, the day of final judgment and the victory of Islam were close, and the apocalyptic events of the Koran cards and sunnah transmissions were taking place in the Middle East. Hence the appeal to the city of Dabiq and victory over the non-believers. When the first issue of the magazine was published, the city was still in the hands of Syrian rebels from the Free Syrian Army. However, as early as August 2014, Islamic State fighters subdued this town of nearly three thousand inhabitants.[12] The symbolic significance of Dabiq ran out with time, and when in October 2016 the soldiers of the Syrian opposition forces[13] assisted by the Turkish army entered the weakly defended city, the magazine has not been published for three months, and was replaced by a new periodical: *Rumiyah.*

Two years after its greatest successes: the seizure of Mosul and Raqqa, the Islamic State lost its initiative. Its expansion was stopped. The Americans supported their allies (the Free Syrian Army and the Iraqi Army) from the air. Support for Assad was sent by Russia, which allowed the

10 This means that the chain of transmitters of a given tradition is authentic and credible, and the content of the message does not conflict with the Koran. Such hadiths are part of the sunnah (which is the Arabic word for traditional customs and practices) and become the basis of Islamic theology and jurisprudence.

11 See https://sunnah.com/muslim/54/44 (14.06.2020).

12 Here in November 2014, an American aid organization employee, Abdul-Rahman Kassig, was murdered. The world has seen a video of the famous British jihadiist Jihadi John threatening the West over Kassig's mutilated body with the panorama of Dabiq in the background. *Dabiq: Why is Syrian Town so Important for IS?*, https://www.bbc.com/news/world-middle-east-30083303 (14.06.2020).

13 *Turkish-backed rebels seize Dabiq from ISIL*, https://www.aljazeera.com/news/2016/10/syria-war-turkish-backed-rebels-seize-dabiq-isil-161016093547972.html (14.06.2020).

Syrian government forces to go on the offensive. Turkish troops crossed the Syrian border fighting ISIS as well as Kurdish fighters. Kurds gradually regained their territories and they were approaching Mosul. Daesh was shrinking, but it still had significant strength in the region and it would hold its both capitals in its hands for over a year. Changes at the front also required changes in propaganda. *Dabiq*, which was initially released about every month, had only three editions in 2016 (last issue on June, 31). Other magazines (*Dar al-Islam*, *Konstantiniyye* and *Istok*) appeared even less regularly. Al-Hayat has decided to stop publishing all of the above titles. On October 5, 2016, a new magazine, *Rumiyah*, appeared on the network. As in the case of *Dabiq*, the title referred to hadith. This time it was a story from the collection of Imam Ahmad Ibn Hanbal, often quoted in the context of jihad. In this hadith,[14] Abdallah, son of Amr Ibn al-As – the famous conqueror of Egypt, asked the Prophet which city would be conquered first: Rome or Constantinople? The Prophet replied that capital of Byzantium would fall the first.[15] Already in the Middle Ages this fragment was noticed.[16] However, it was only after the capture of Constantinople by the Turks in 1453 that it gained new significance. Now this hadith became the promise of the conquest of Rome (Rumiya), a symbol of Western civilization.[17] New goal – new title. Of course, the fact that at the time of the issue of *Rumiyah*'s first issue, the Syrian rebels and the Turkish army were preparing an offensive towards Dabiq and the city was impossible to save. This also forced a change in the title of the flagship ISIS magazine.[18]

Rumiyah has become the only magazine presenting the Islamic State's point of view. It still remained an extremely useful and needed recruitment tool, which is why Al-Hayat decided to expand its audience. It was published mainly in English, but this time it was accompanied by more language versions. In addition to the Arabic, German and French versions already known from *Dabiq*, translations into Bosnian, Bahasa, Uighur, Pashto, Turkish and Urdu have also appeared. This indicates a much more ambitious plans of the founders of the magazine, but at the same time the extension and internationalization of the subject. Stopping the expansion

---

14 "Rumiyah", No. 1, p. 38.

15 Literally: the city of Heraclius.

16 K.A. Goudie, *Reinventing Jihād: Jihād Ideology From the Conquest of Jerusalem to the end of the Ayyūbids (c. 492/1099–647/1249)*, Brill, Leiden 2019, pp. 109–111.

17 ISIS called its opponents Crusaders, hence the great symbolic significance of Rome.

18 M. Comerford, *What ISIS lost in Dabiq*, https://www.newstatesman.com/politics/staggers/2016/10/what-isis-lost-dabiq (14.06.2020)

in Syria and Iraq has shifted the focus not only on propagating hijra but also on conducting attacks in the US, Europe and even such places as Kenya or Bangladesh.[19] There are also guides, rarely found in *Dabiq*, but characteristic for *Inspire*, how to carry out an assassination, how to attack with a knife or advice on taking hostages.[20]

Contrary to the efforts of the propaganda department, the reality of Islamic State was not optimistic. Daesh's territory was rapidly shrinking and the members of the organization were becoming increasingly dispersed. Al-Hayat managed to publish 13 issues before being forced to close the *Rumiyah* project. The last issue was released on September 9, 2017. A month and a half earlier, the Iraqi regained Mosul, a month later, American-backed Syrian rebels drove Daesh fighters out of Raqqa. ISIS in the Middle East was losing its last territories, but it continued to operate in secret and in virtual space.

Feminine jihad

Internet magazines were addressed primarily to men. Their main goals were the recruitment of new fighters, assistance in the organization of attacks and the building of bonds of brotherhood and community. Reporting of subsequent skirmishes, discussing techniques of terrorist attacks or interviews with known fighters were to tempt young men (and boys) to join the ranks of supporters of Al-Qaeda or Islamic State. The first attempt to create a magazine addressed to women was made by the Al Qaeda's Women Information Bureau of the Arabian Peninsula. In 2004, the first issue of the *Al-Khansa* magazine dedicated to women was released. The magazine, entirely published in Arabic, contained articles addressed to mujahedin wives and mothers.

The magazine's title referred to the figure of the well-known poet from the Jahiliyyah period and early Islam – Al-Khansa Tumāḍir bint ʿAmr ibn al-Ḥārith ibn al-Sharīd al-Sulamīyah from the Banu Sulaym. The prophet's peer became famous for her touching elegies written after the death

19 R.J. Bunker, P. Ligouri-Bunker, *The Islamic State English-Language Online Magazine Rumiyah (Rome)*, http://www.terrorism.org/wp-content/uploads/2019/08/Rumiyah_eBook_web.pdf (14.06.2020).

20 Section "Just Terror Tactics" in the 2nd, 3rd, 5th, and the 9th issue of *Rumiya*.

of her beloved brothers Mu'awiyyah and Sakhr, who were killed in tribal feuds.[21] Despite the successes at the annual poetic struggles accompanying the Ukaz fairs, it was not her mastery of word that won the hearts of modern jihadists. Al-Khansa in the "Year of Messages" (629) came to Medina to meet Mohammed as one of her tribe's representatives. She converted to Islam and became its fervent advocate. Muslim tradition says that she followed her six sons from one battlefield to another when they took part in the triumphal march of the Islamic army during the great conquests. Four of them were killed in a key battle with the Sassanid army at Qadisiya. Al-Khansa received the news of their death calmly and expressed thanks to God for giving them such a glorious death and hope that after her death she would be able to join them in Paradise.[22] "Mother of martyrs" has become a model of the perfect woman, wife and mother for jihad apologists.

The first of the women's jihadist magazines was quite economical in form and was amateurish. The main emphasis was placed on the content, completely giving up illustrations and photos, leaving only modest ornaments at the bottom of the page. The articles called for women to participate in jihad.[23] First of all, the role of fighters' wives and mothers was anticipated for them. The active participation of women in combat was approached with some caution. This was allowed, but only as a last resort. It was assumed that when jihad became the personal duty of every Muslim, women should also take part in it and no man could forbid them.[24] This ambiguous attitude reflects a certain difference of views that arose at that time between the main leaders of Al-Qaeda. On the one hand, the leader of

---

21 F. Gabrielli, *Al-Khansa*, in: E. van Donzel, B. Lewis et al. (eds.), *Encyclopaedia of Islam*, Vol. 4, Brill, Leiden 1997, p. 1027.

22 N.M. El Cheikh, *Women, Islam, and Abbasid Identity*, Harvard University Press, Cambridge 2015, pp. 115–116.

23 The entire magazine can easily be found online, and the fragments translated into English were posted by Middle East Media Research Institute. *Al-Qa'ida Women's Magazine: Women Must Participate in Jihad*, https://www.memri.org/reports/al-qaida-womens-magazine-women-must-participate-jihad (15.06.2020).

24 Such position was taken from the writings of Abdullah Azzam – one of the creators of Al-Qaida. Not only creators of Al-Khansa were inspired by the words of this jihad ideologist. Already in 1988, the Islamic Resistance Movement Hamas included an almost literal quote from Azzam, in its statutory document, in article 12 of the charter: "Fighting the enemy becomes the individual obligation of every Muslim man and woman. The woman is allowed to go fight without permission of her husband and slave without the permission of his master". T. Hegghammer, *The Caravan. Abdallah Azzam and the Rise of Global Jihad*, Cambridge University Press, Cambridge 2020, pp 382–383; M. Maqdsi, *Charter of the Islamic Resistance Movement (Hamas) of Palestine*, "Journal of Palestine Studies" 1993, Vol. 22, No. 4, p. 125.

the organization in Iraq and one of the inspirators of the later Islamic State, Abu Musab az-Zarqawi, encouraged women to actively participate in the holy war against infidels. On the other hand, then number two in Al-Qaeda (after Osama bin Laden), and today's leader, Egyptian Ayman az-Zawahiri, believed that women should not leave home and focus on raising children and supporting their male relatives in their fight.[25]

Although widely commented, *Al-Khansa* did not achieve the expected success. In 2010, the magazine *Hafidat al-Khansa* (Granddaughters of Al-Khansa) appeared, thanks to the Samud agency. Despite being mentioned by analysts and researchers on the topic of jihadist propaganda, it also failed to break through to a wider audience. The magazine's layout was more modern than its predecessors. Photos appeared next to the articles, but it still visually looked more like a traditional newspaper than a modern women's magazine. Similarly, *Al-Shamikha* (Majestic Woman) presented itself on the cover as "a female Islamist jihadist magazine". Quickly defined in the west by the term "Jihad Cosmo", it still left much to be desired from the visual side. The originators tried to reach readers in various ways. One of the ideas was entrusting women's articles to women. However, the topics included were quite inconsistent. Inside, next to the article on the upbringing of sons into real *mujahideen*, there were also tips on the beauty and use of honey masks.[26] Arabic-language online magazines have not managed to exert such an influence on women as their creators assumed, imitating Western women's magazines in the style of Cosmopolitan or Elle. They never went beyond electronic distribution, which significantly reduced the reach of the magazines.[27]

---

25 In 2008, Az-Zawahiri stated, that "Al-Qaeda has no women, but the women of the mujahideen do their heroic part in taking care of their homes and sons in the roughness of the immigration, movement, unity, and expecting the Crusader strikes". A. Perešin, *The Role of Women in post-IS Jihadist Transformation*, in: J. Leman, Ş. Pektaş (eds.), *Militant Jihadism: Today and Tomorrow*, Leuven University Press, Leuven 2019, pp. 103–104; *The Role of Women in Jihad*, Insite Blog on Terrorism and Extremism, https://news.siteintelgroup.com/blog/index.php/about-us/21-jihad/41-feb09-sp-102064454 (15.06.2020).

26 H. Fraihi, *The Future of Feminism by ISIS is in the Lap of Women*, "International Annals of Criminology" 2018, No. 56, p. 24.

27 Esther Solis Al-Tabaa conducted an interesting analysis of the first issue of *Al-Shamikha* in her article. In it, she recognized that such activities could bring measurable benefits for Al-Qaeda. In retrospect, however, it looks different. The short range, limited to Arabic only, and inconsistent message have caused Al-Qaeda to lose its initiative for the Islamic State media apparatus regarding propaganda impact on women. E.S. Al-Tabaa, *Targeting a Female Audience: American Muslim Women's Perceptions of al-Qaida Propaganda*, "Journal of Strategic Security" 2013, Vol. 6, No. 3 Suppl., pp. 10–21.

Al-Hayat Media Center responsible for media service and propagating the idea of Islamic State has not decided to create a magazine addressed directly to women along the lines of Al-Qaeda. This does not mean, however, that they did not address this topic in their press publications. *Dabiq* was the perfect platform to address potential women fighters. The magazine's main propaganda goal was to encourage volunteers from Europe and the English-speaking world to emigrate to the territories occupied by Daesh. Women as potential wives and mothers of jihadists also were in the orbit of the magazine's editors interests. In the seventh issue of the magazine, which appeared on February 12, 2015, for the first time appeared the column *To Our Sisters*. The short, two-page interview was widely commented on by the global media. Its heroine was Umm Basir al-Muhajirah, formerly known as Hayat Boumeddiene and hailed in early 2015 as France's most wanted woman. Her husband Amedy Coulibaly (Abu Basir al-Ifriqi) on January 8, 2015, shot a policewoman in Paris, Clarissa Jean-Philippe, then pursued by the police, broke into a Jewish Hypercacher supermarket at Porte de Vincennes district, killed four men who tried to stop him and took 15 hostages. He claimed that the attack on the Jewish store was revenge for the actions of the Syrian government and the Western coalition against Muslims in Syria, Iraq, Mali and Afghanistan. In negotiations with the police, he demanded security for the Kouachi brothers, terrorist who shot 12 people two days earlier in the editorial office of the satirical weekly *Charlie Hebdo*. The brothers were hiding from a police raid and also took hostages in Dammartin-en-Goële. The French commandos were afraid that there would be more victims and stormed the supermarket. Coulibaly was shot and the hostages saved. At the same time, officers of the French special services GIGN shot Said and Cherif Kouachi.[28]

According to the French services, Hayat Boumeddiene was actively involved in the preparations for the attack. On January 2, she and her husband left for Madrid, from there she flew to Istanbul and managed to get to Syria. She crossed the border on January 8.[29] Western intelligence services tried unsuccessfully for a month to trace her. A month later, *Dabiq* published its interview with Boumeddiene and an Islamist propaganda

---

[28] *Charlie Hebdo Attack: Three Days of Terror*, https://www.bbc.com/news/world-europe-30708237 (16.06.2020).

[29] E. Thomas, *Who is Hayat Boumeddiene?*, http://www.bbc.co.uk/newsbeat/article/30760975/who-is-hayat-boumeddiene (16.06.2020).

magazine appeared in all major Western news sites. A young woman who spent a difficult childhood in foster families and only after marrying Coulibaly converted to Islam, now she became a jihadist celebrity. The interview was not a typical conversation. Umm Basir answered only a few questions, and her answers were carefully prepared to match them with the coherent message that *Dabiq* promoted. Islamic State as the heir to the thoughts of Abu Musab az-Zarqawi looked favorably at the direct participation of women in jihad.[30] However, *Dabiq* itself was more conservative in this respect. Boumeddiene told about her husband, his willingness to make a *hijra* and a sense of duty to "perform an operation in France". At the end she gave a message to Muslim sisters. They should support their husbands, make all matters easier for them. They are to be strong and bold, focused on the goal and not waste time on idle fun.

What is significant that the accounts of Hayat herself before her escape from France and the photos from the beginning of her relationship with Coulibaly show a rather liberal approach to conservative Muslim values. She appealed to ISIS supporters to learn religion and read the Quran. She referred to Mariam (mother of Jesus), who is an example of purity, modesty and obedience in Islam. The message that was put in the mouth of Umm Basir is simple and clearly laid out: a woman is first and foremost to be an obedient and supportive wife.[31]

Starting from the seventh issue, already mentioned, in the next seven editions of *Dabiq* a special section for women appears, entitled *To Our Sisters* (Nos. 7, 8, 11, 12 and 13) or *From Our Sisters* (Nos. 9 and 10). The author of the next six articles is the mysterious Umm Sumayyah al-Muhajirah. She reveals little about herself in her texts. We know that she is an Arab who has made a *hijra* to Islamic State. She mentions, however, that during her travels she was the only Arab among other women, so she probably came to Daesh from one of the European countries. She certainly received a very solid religious education. Her articles are interspersed with

---

30 An examples are the famous female brigades Umm al-Rayyan and Al-Khansa. An another interesting example may also be the character of Aqsa Mahmood, a Scottish Muslim who joined ISIS in 2013 at the age of 20. Aqsa posed for photos with a machine gun, and on her twitter microblogging and social networking service she posted reports of violent executions. Some commentators accused her of inspiring so-called Jihadi Brides, girls who went to Syria and Iraq in search of husbands and a more adventurous lifestyle. A. Fantz, A. Shubert, *From Scottish Teen to ISIS Bride and Recruiter: The Aqsa Mahmood Story*, https://edition.cnn.com/2015/02/23/world/scottish-teen-isis-recruiter/index.html (16.06.2020).

31 "Dabiq", No. 7, pp. 50–52.

quotes from the Quran and sunna.[32] Umm Sumayyah raises very controversial topics like sexual slavery, jihad duty, and polygamy. Her argument is deeply rooted in Sharia law, specifically understood by Salafi jihadists. She writes in a style that doesn't allow discussion and doubt. She is firm and convinced of her arguments. Her texts are an interpretation of the ideology of the Islamic State. She presents a masculine misogynist point of view and considers it to be the only valid vision of social order.[33]

In her first article, *The Twin Halves of the Muhajirin*, Umm Sumayyah focuses on the necessity of *hijra*. She supports the lengthy argument with Quran verses (Arabic: آية āyah, plural آيات āyāt) and specific hadiths. She wants to prove, based on the Salafi interpretation of Sharia, that the escape of the land of non-believers (dārul-kufr),[34] where Muslims are persecuted, and just being in a place where divine law is not respected can lead to "death of heart", to the country of Islam (dārul-Islam) is the duty of every believer. This also applies to women because, according to Prophet Muhammad in the hadith quoted by the author, "a woman is a twin half of a man".[35] Then, she refutes the allegations that ISIS opponents have made against expatriates. She rejects the narrative of western nationalist circles that immigrants and their families are a social margin and an uneducated poor. She builds in her women-readers a sense that they are unique and that only in the lands controlled by Daesh they will be appreciated. She tries to dispel the doubts of potential recruits. She knows that the attitude of parents and other relatives can be a serious obstacle for young Muslim women.[36]

She makes fun of the argument that a woman "fleeing" to Islamic State is jeopardizing her honor. In her eyes, a much greater threat to the worship of a Muslim woman is to go to study in London or Paris. She categorically states that during *jihad*, a woman should ignore the opinion of loved ones

---

32 Always with reference to a specific collection of hadiths. This indicates a good theological education, not just a practical knowledge of tradition.

33 We can't rule out that Umm Sumayyah is just a virtual character created by propaganda specialists.

34 Such an entry is used by the author herself.

35 This hadith is confirmed in at least three collections: Ibn Majah, At-Tirmidhi and Abu Dawud, "Dabiq", No. 8, p. 33.

36 This was the case with the already mentioned Aqsa Mahmood. Her parents, after her escape, repeatedly called for her return, but at the same time accused her in the press of treason and breaking up the family. *Parents of IS-linked Aqsa Mahmood Feel 'Betrayed'*, https://www.bbc.com/news/uk-scotland-glasgow-west-29048536 (18.06.2020).

and even without a male guardian (*mahram*) attempt a *hijra*. Then she gives the stories of women immigrants who sacrificed a lot to reach Syria. Pregnant women and old women who, against all odds, got to *dārul-Islam*. Of course, we can't verify the truth of these stories, but that's not the point Umm Sumayyah. These stories are to convince hesitating readers to make a decision to escape. Descriptions are becoming more and more lofty and pathetic, culminating in her own memories of tears and joy at the sight of the flag of the Islamic State waving over the post manned by Daesh soldiers. At the end Umm Sumayyah decides to settle accounts with the internal enemy. The last words are directed to supporters of Abu Muhammad al-Maqdisi[37] gathered around the portal Minbar at-Tawhīd wal-Jihād.[38] Without mincing words, Umm Sumayyah accused them of cowardice and lack of manhood.[39] This ending disturbs the message directed to the "sisters", but allows us to look behind the scenes of the internal dispute between different branches of the jihadist movement.[40]

In the ninth issue of *Dabiq*, which was released on May 21, 2015, Umm Sumayyah posted another article. The response was unique, and comments spread all over the world. In August last year, Islamic State soldiers captured the city of Sinjar in Iraqi Kurdistan, inhabited largely by Yazidis.[41] The inhabitants of the city were in hell. Several thousand Yazidis were murdered. Furthermore, many women and children were kidnapped and divided among Daesh fighters as slaves. Public opinion, also in the Muslim world, was shocked by this barbarism. Umm Sumayyah decided to resist these accusations. Her article *Slave-Girls or Prostitutes* begins with

---

37 One of the leading ideologists of global jihad. He is considered the spiritual father of Abu Musab az-Zarqawi. However, their paths diverged. Maqdisi did not support his student's radicalism. ISIS did not find his approval either. He condemned the actions of the Islamic State, especially in the event of the burning of a captured Jordanian pilot in January 2015. His attitude ensured him release from Jordanian prison and undying hatred on the part of Daesh.

38 Currently (June 2020), only the Arabic version of the portal is available; http://www.ilmway.com/site/maqdis/MS_76.html. Extremely popular English version of this site: http://tawhed.ws has been "under construction" for a long time.

39 Literally: „May Allah disfigure the turbans of the PKK's women, yet they have more manhood than your likes!", "Dabiq", No. 8, p. 37.

40 B. Lia, *The Jihādī Movement and Rebel Governance: A Reassertion of a Patriarchal Order?*, "Die Welt des Islams" 2017, No. 57, pp. 467–468.

41 One of the Middle East religious minorities. Yazidism is a syncretic religion, combining elements of Islam, Christianity and Zoroastrianism. Importantly, they are not considered "people of the book" (ahl-al-kitab), which Muslims are obliged to protect (in practice to tolerate only) by the Quran and the sunna. Ethnically, Yazidis are Kurds.

numerous references to the Quran and sunna. The author proves that having sex with slaves is allowed for orthodox Muslims (as opposed to prostitution). Laws dating back to the early days of Islam's expansion have long been no longer used in the modern Arab world. Umm Sumayyah argues, however, that since the caliphate has been renewed, the old laws generally recognized as inhumane should be re-implemented. Interspersed with Quran verses (ayahs) and hadiths, the author's tirade is a polemic with a critical opinion from other Muslims. According to Umm Sumayyah, both slavery (*saby*) and sexual exploitation of slaves (*tassari*) are not only allowed, but recommended by Sharia. They serve the humiliation of the defeated and are an expression of Islam's triumph over infidels.[42] In an argument full of venom and malice, the author mocks modern Muslims. He accuses them of turning away from Islam, expresses pride in the creation of the caliphate by force and the seizure of infidels. She directly strikes the rulers of Saudi Arabia, Qatar and the UAE by calling them *taghut*,[43] suggesting that they renounced God and called them "White House foster children". Not acknowledging slavery is giving up faith. In the eyes of Umm Sumayyah, rape on slaves[44] is definitely less evil than using the services of prostitutes, which she considers to be women without reverence and honor. Finally, the author is just comparing the wife of the US President, Michelle Obama to the prostitute.

While in the first article from the eighth issue the propaganda goal of the article was clear and obvious, it is more difficult to indicate the recipient of this repulsive material here. Importantly, this time the Umm Sumayyah's column is titled *From Our Sisters* instead of *To Our Sisters*. This could suggest that *Slave-Girls or Prostitutes* is supposed to present a woman's point of view, but it is not necessarily aimed at women. However, editors are not consistent here. In the 10th issue, despite retaining the new title of the column, Umm Sumayyah returns to propaganda rhetoric aimed at Muslim women. Moreover, to a precisely defined group of women. The article *They Are Not Lawful Spouses for One Another* is addressed to the

---

[42] "Therefore, we did not humiliate them, but it was Allah who did so at the hands of His truthful slaves who did not wish for anything except for Allah's word to be supreme and the kuffār's words to be lowest. For that sake, they have exerted their souls and hearts. Their aim is sublimity for the religion and humiliation of whoever desires a religion other than Islam!". Umm Sumayyah, "Dabiq", No. 9, p. 46.

[43] The term used today in the sense of a tyrant, a person who does not obey divine law, often under the cultural influence of Western civilization.

[44] Umm Sumayyah doesn't use the term 'rape'.

wives of Sahwa[45] soldiers, Arab opponents of ISIS in Syria and Iraq. The methods of persuasion in this case are no different from the classic arsenal of Umm Sumayyah's arguments. The religious argument comes first. The main thesis put forward by the author is the fact that members of Sahwat, when opposed to Islamic State, abandoned Islam. Since they became apostates, marriage vows became irrelevant, their wives should abandon them and make hijra in Daesh territory. Fear of poverty, scarcity, and family anger should not be an excuse. Moreover, being in such a relationship is a sin of adultery (*zina*),[46] one of the greatest offenses against divine law. So, no need to wait for other women, you need to take the first step and act.

Umm Sumayyah's manipulation here is characteristic of the Salafi jihadist doctrine of Islam. *Takfir*, or recognition as unfaithful, allows ISIS leaders to exclude entire Muslim groups from the community of believers. Initially used mainly against Shiites, along with the development of the idea and territory of the Islamic State, it was used more and more often. After such a declaration, ISIS members could feel relieved of any doubts they might have about fighting the brothers in faith.[47]

The 11th issue of *Dabiq* and the next article by Umm Sumayyah appeared on September 9, 2015. The peak of the territorial expansion of caliphate fell in May this year. From now on, Daesh will gradually lose the conquered land, and more actors will be involved in the fight against Islamic State. In September, the position of the terrorist state was still strong. Umm Sumayyah raised the topic of women's participation in the holy war

---

45 Sahwa (Awakening) is a Sunni militia (actually militias, sahwat) sponsored by the US. Established in 2006 as a counterweight to the so-called Al-Qaeda in Iraq, which under Az-Zarqawi, destabilized American forces in Iraq and its supportive government in Baghdad. Over time, the Sahwat lost their importance. In ISIS propaganda, however, this term is also used to describe all supporters of the Iraqi government, and Umm Sumayyah uses this term for all Sunni Daesh opponents, like the Iraqi army or the Free Syrian Army. A. Khaleel, *The Future of the Iraqi Sunni Arabs*, in: A. Khaleel, J. Eriksson (eds.), *Iraq after ISIS: The Challenges of Post-War Recovery*, Springer, Cham 2018, pp. 48–50.

46 *Zina*, depending on the legal school, may define a much larger category of sins than adultery, including prostitution, rape, sodomy, and homosexuality. It is also one of the deeds that are threatened with punishments established directly in the Quran (*hudud*). The accusation of Umm Summayyah against the addressees of the article was therefore really serious.

47 The modern concept of *takfir* so readily used by Salafists and its historical roots describes Shiraz Maher very well. He draws attention to the fact that this term has been experiencing a kind of renaissance since 2003, when Az-Zarqawi and his supporters began to use it in relation to Shiites. S. Maher, *Salafi-Jihadism. The History of the Idea*, Oxford University Press, Oxford 2016, pp. 69–107.

against infidels this time. She already wrote earlier about this, however, ISIS propagandists came to the conclusion that the topic needs further development. *A Jihad without Fighting* is a text in which we can easily recognize the characteristic Umm Sumayyah's style. Again, what we get is, interwoven with quotes from the Quran and sunna, theological argumentation using very simple but also effective propaganda tricks.

The author begins by stating that Islam does not require women to participate directly in jihad, except for defense against attack. However, this does not mean that Muslim women have no other duties associated with holy war. "I write this article for my Muslim sister, the wife of a mujāhid and the mother of lion cubs".[48] Umm Sumayyah writes and clearly defines what tasks Daesh puts before her women citizens. In addition to quoting extensive fragments of *tafsir* by Ibn Kathir,[49] the author also plays on the emotions of the women readers. She describes a fighter who was captured and his wife turned away from him. She condemns such behavior to show in a moment the right way that women of Islamic State should follow. Patience, dedication and focus on the education of subsequent generations of fighters. She calls her readers lionesses, and their children lion cubs, who in time will become soldiers of the Caliphate. Giving life and raising children in the ideals of Islamic State is the most important task of truly faithful Muslim women, mocking a Western approach on this issue. Instead of the stories of Cinderella or Robin Hood, they must put heroes of Islam as an example for their kids, stories from the Quran and hadith. Only in the lands of caliphate women can get support in the form of training camps or special kindergartens for ISIS lion cubs. Positive and negative examples are to convince readers of the importance of their role. They help to find a goal in life and increase self-respect.

The last of Umm Sumayyah's articles was published in the 12th issue of November 2015, entitled *Two, Three, or Four* which focuses on the issue of polygyny. For many European women, and they were the main goal of *Dabiq*'s propaganda, polygamy was one of the issues that could discourage them from *hijra*. Umm Sumayyah tries to explain to readers that such practices are the most right because they are religiously sanctioned. In addition, she tries to rationalize the institution of polygamy. Her arguments,

---

48 "Dabiq", No. 11, p. 41.

49 Ibn Kathir's tafsir is one of the most known and most commonly used commentary on the Quran. The author is a 14th-century jurist, theologian and historian from Damascus, Ismaʿil Ibn ʿUmar Ibn Kathir.

however, present a decidedly male point of view. A second wife is necessary when the first one, for various reasons, cannot fulfill her marriage obligations. Similarly, in a situation where one of the wives is infertile, a man can take another without rejecting the former. These arguments are not very convincing, and Umm Sumayyah quickly moves on to the proven practice of scoffing at opponents, stating that the criticism of polygyny results from nothing more than the jealousy of women.

The situation of the Islamic State has become increasingly difficult since the end of 2015, and *Dabiq* is issued irregularly. In the 13th issue a short article written in sublime style about experiencing the mourning of the deceased husband is addressed "to the sisters". There is no sign of the author of the text under it. The style, similar to Umm Sumayyah, however, is devoid of rhetoric fierce, propaganda tricks and mocking characteristic of this author. Number 14 has no female column at all. However, in the last, 15th issue of *Dabiq* one of the most interesting texts addressed to women from ISIS press materials appeared. *How I Came to Islam* by Umm Khalid al-Finladiyyah is a memory of *muhajira* who came to Syria from Finland.[50] We are not dealing with a Muslim from birth as in the case of Boumeddiene or Umm Sumayyah. Umm Khalid is a neophyte who was born in a Protestant family in secularized Finland, as she recalls, where religion is only superficial. She describes her path to Islam from youthful rebellion, by undermining religious dogmas (an incomprehensible Trinity) and scientific truths (unclear theories of evolution and the big bang) to joining a small Muslim community in Helsinki. Readers – potential recruits could identify with her story.

The author does not abuse theological terminology, demonstrates understanding and evokes a sense of community. The decision to make a *hijra* was influenced by the arrest of her husband suspected of terrorist activities. When they managed to get him out of prison, they decided to leave for Syria. She writes about initial difficulties, ignorance of the language, change of lifestyle. She arouses the sympathy and liking of its recipients. However, she does not forget what the purpose of its publication is. It's about persuading hesitating Muslim women to go to Daesh. So after describing the hardships of travel and acclimatization, from the story of Umm

---

[50] According to a report by Finnish intelligence services, at least 70 adult Finnish citizens joined ISIS by the end of 2015. *"Finnish Woman" Tells Propaganda Magazine how She Joined Isis*, https://www.helsinkitimes.fi/finland/finland-news/domestic/14144-finnish-woman-tells-propaganda-magazine-how-she-joined-isis.html (29.06.2020).

Khalid, begins to emerge the vision of a country that has become a reward for all overcome adversities. In Caliphate, life is clean and children are not exposed to the harmful effects of Satan as in *dar al-kufr* (the land of infidels). Even when her son died in a fight, Al-Finlandiyyah receives this as another blessing. It would be better for him to die in God's path than to live outside Caliphate. She ends her article with an appeal addressed directly to women that they should not hesitate and make *hijra*. In contrast, those that cannot get to Syria and Iraq should "to attack the Crusaders and their allies wherever you are, as that is something that you are able to do".[51] And this statement is a certain novelty, perhaps related to the fact that in 2016 (number 15 appeared at the end of July) ISIS lost the initiative, and the scales of war were already tipping in favor of Daesh's opponents.

Rumiyah, which replaced *Dabiq*, was published for a year between September 2016 and September 2017. At that time, Daesh was losing its territory. In July 2017, Mosul fell into the hands of the Iraqi army, and three months later the fighters had to leave their capital in Raqqa. The propaganda message has also changed. The call for *hijra* was gradually replaced by orders to attack the infidels on their territory. Articles addressed to women also looked different. Each of the 13 issues contained a text addressed to Muslim women,[52] but these articles lost their propaganda character. They concerned issues related to family and spiritual life. Examples of women, mainly from the first years of Islam, were supposed to become role models for contemporary people. The topics of steadfastness, modesty and marital fidelity were discussed, among others. Practical advice was given on how to behave in a mosque, how to raise children. Women were called to stay at home, support their husbands, keep secrets etc. All appeals were supported by numerous quotations from the Quran, collections of hadiths and Islamic history. On the other hand, we hardly find calls for *hijra* and intrusive propaganda so common in *Dabiq*.

Several factors could have contributed to this. First of all, the worsening situation at the front. When the Islamic State triumphed and conquered more regions of Iraq and Syria, potential women candidates could have deluded themselves that Caliphate would settle in the Middle East for longer. In 2017, the fate of ISIS was already numbered, and driving his fighters out

[51] "Dabiq", No. 15, p. 39.

[52] In numbers 5, 6, 10 and 11 this column was entitled *Sisters*. In these and other cases, women's articles were characterized by a different, more "feminine" layout with floral ornaments and matching illustrations of women militants or children.

of the major cities of Syria and Iraq was a matter of time. Not only would it be difficult to get to Daesh branches, but maintaining and organizing your stay for volunteers would be impossible with shrinking state finances and disorganized administration. Despite many similarities, *Rumiyah* had a slightly different purpose than *Dabiq*. This is demonstrated, inter alia, by the increase in the number of language versions. The first magazine was published primarily in English, and other European languages were only a supplement. The second one, from the beginning appeared in Arabic, but also in Bahasa and Urdu. So it became available to a huge audience in Muslim Asian countries such as Pakistan and Indonesia. Ipso facto, the profile of readers has changed. In *Rumiyah*'s editors' view, explaining religious issues or interpreting Islamic principles in a jihadist spirit became more important than recruitment and propaganda. Arabic terms such as *ʿaqida* (justice), *tawhid* (monotheism), *wala wa bara* (support and condemnation), *taghut* (tyranny), etc. are more commonly used, typical of Salafi writings and speeches. It was assumed that the recipients would be Muslim women. As the next paragraph will show, the addressees will often be women from Islamic State.

Of all *Rumiyah's* "feminine" texts, two are the most important for our considerations. One in the eleventh issue entitled *Our Journey to Allah* is an interpretation of the Islamic State's position on women. At the same time, it is an appeal to remind the reader of the values and goals set for Muslim women. The anonymous author[53] at the beginning notes: "I invite my sisters in the Islamic State who – by Allah's grace – have remaining firm, patient and persevering, to lend me their ears, as I believe we are in serious need of reminders and rectification".[54] So it's not about recruitment and propaganda. In a pathetic style, the author lists the characteristics that an ISIS woman-member should have, which can be summarized with one quote: "Let us be as those women who knew their role and fulfilled them, for being supportive of your mujahid husband is one of your key roles in the land of jihad, my dear sister, and the importance of it cannot be overemphasized".[55] The author often uses phrases such as; we women, we Muslims. This is a very simple rhetorical procedure that allows readers to identify more strongly with the theses of the article.

[53] With the exception of one (from number 13), all texts addressed to women are anonymous.

[54] "Rumiyah", No. 11, p. 12.

[55] Ibid., p. 14.

The second article standing out from the others in *Rumiyah*, is *The Hijrah of Umm Sulaym al-Muhajirah* from the last, 13th issue of the magazine. This is the only one from the series of "female" texts whose author we know by name. Umm Sulaym is an Australian who infiltrated ISIS controlled areas in 2014. The text is quite a detailed account of this journey. Umm Sulaym's husband died in January 2014. She and her children, despite the family's opposition, managed to get to Turkey from where, overcoming many difficulties, she crossed the border and found herself on ISIS territory. The text is equally addressed to women and men. It focuses more on political disputes than on persuading to follow the author's footsteps.

The author points out the enemies of ISIS (including Jabhat an-Nusra, Turkey, Sahwat militia, Free Syrian Army) and arouses the anger of readers moved by the fate of Umm Sulaym. Much has changed since Umm Sumayyah published her articles. The article is no longer triumphalistic, it does not encourage *hijra*, it does not recruit new members. There is an atmosphere of tension and preparation for the defense of the last bastion. "And let these Crusaders take heed, for just as the Khilafah is filled with men who love death more than the Crusaders love life, likewise are the women of the Islamic State. So let them not think that we will succumb due to them targeting our husbands with drones, or bombing our homes, or dropping white phosphorus on our children. Well! This only strengthens our conviction, inshaallah".[56] A month after the publication of these words, Raqqa will collapse.

Both *Dabiq* and *Rumiyah* were important news channels that Islamic State propaganda used to the extent that they became its symbol. The magazines were often commented on in the Western media, which made them reach a very large audience. We cannot estimate how large a group of women they have influenced. How many of them have become convinced to make *hijra* by reading these magazines. We cannot, of course, overestimate them, they were important, but only one of the modes of the extremely extensive Al-Hayat Media Center propaganda machine. Materials addressed to women were steeped in Salafi ideology and allowed to better understand what role they were to play in a kind of jihadist utopia which the Islamic State was to be.

---

56 "Rumiyah", No. 13, p. 35.

References

Al-Qa'ida Women's Magazine: Women Must Participate in Jihad, https://www.memri.org/reports/al-qaida-womens-magazine-women-must-participate-jihad (15.06.2020).

Al-Tabaa E.S., *Targeting a Female Audience: American Muslim Women's Perceptions of al-Qaida Propaganda*, "Journal of Strategic Security" 2013, Vol. 6, No. 3 Suppl., pp. 10–21.

Bunker R.J., Ligouri-Bunker P., *The Islamic State English-Language Online Magazine Rumiyah (Rome)*, http://www.terrorism.org/wp-content/uploads/2019/08/Rumiyah_eBook_web.pdf (14.06.2020).

Charlie Hebdo Attack: Three Days of Terror, https://www.bbc.com/news/world-europe-30708237 (16.06.2020).

Comerford M., *What ISIS Lost in Dabiq*, https://www.newstatesman.com/politics/staggers/2016/10/what-isis-lost-dabiq (14.06.2020).

Cook J., Vale G., *From Daesh to 'Diaspora': Tracing the Women and Minors of Islamic State*, https://icsr.info/wp-content/uploads/2018/07/Women-in-ISIS-report_20180719_web.pdf (01.07.2020).

Dabiq: Why is Syrian Town so Important for IS?, https://www.bbc.com/news/world-middle-east-30083303 (14.06.2020).

El Cheikh N.M., *Women, Islam, and Abbasid Identity*, Harvard University Press, Cambridge 2015.

Fantz A., Shubert A., *From Scottish Teen to ISIS Bride and Recruiter: The Aqsa Mahmood Story*, https://edition.cnn.com/2015/02/23/world/scottish-teen-isis-recruiter/index.html (16.06.2020).

"Finnish woman" Tells Propaganda Magazine how She Joined Isis, https://www.helsinkitimes.fi/finland/finland-news/domestic/14144-finnish-woman-tells-propaganda-magazine-how-she-joined-isis.html (29.06.2020).

Fraihi H., *The Future of Feminism by ISIS is in the Lap of Women*, "International Annals of Criminology" 2018, No. 56, p. 24.

Gabrielli F., *Al-Khansa*, in: E. van Donzel, B. Lewis et al. (eds.), *Encyclopaedia of Islam*, Vol. 4, Brill, Leiden 1997.

Gambhir H.K., *Dabiq: The Strategic Messaging of the Islamic State*, http://www.understandingwar.org/sites/default/files/Dabiq%20Backgrounder_Harleen%20Final_0.pdf (13.06.2020).

Goudie K.A., *Reinventing Jihād: Jihād Ideology From the Conquest of Jerusalem to the end of the Ayyūbids (c. 492/1099–647/1249)*, Brill, Leiden 2019.

Hegghammer T., *The Caravan. Abdallah Azzam and the Rise of Global Jihad*, Cambridge University Press, Cambridge 2020.

Khaleel A., *The Future of the Iraqi Sunni Arabs*, in: A. Khaleel, J. Eriksson (eds.), *Iraq after ISIS: The Challenges of Post-War Recovery*, Springer, Cham 2018.

Lia B., *The Jihādī Movement and Rebel Governance: A Reassertion of a Patriarchal Order?*, "Die Welt des Islams" 2017, No. 57.

Maher S., *Salafi-Jihadism. The History of the Idea*, Oxford University Press, Oxford 2016.

Maqdsi M., *Charter of the Islamic Resistance Movement (Hamas) of Palestine*, "Journal of Palestine Studies" 1993, Vol. 22, No. 4.

Parents of IS-linked Aqsa Mahmood Feel 'Betrayed', https://www.bbc.com/news/uk-scotland-glasgow-west-29048536 (18.06.2020).

Perešin A., *The Role of Women in post-IS Jihadist Transformation*, in: J. Leman, Ş. Pektaş *(eds.), Militant Jihadism: Today and Tomorrow*, Leuven University Press, Leuven 2019.

The Role of Women in Jihad, Insite Blog on Terrorism and Extremism, https://news.siteintelgroup.com/blog/index.php/about-us/21-jihad/41-feb09-sp-102064454 (15.06.2020).

Thomas E., *Who is Hayat Boumeddiene?*, http://www.bbc.co.uk/newsbeat/article/30760975/who-is-hayat-boumeddiene (16.06.2020).

Turkish-backed rebels seize Dabiq from ISIL, https://www.aljazeera.com/news/2016/10/syria-war-turkish-backed-rebels-seize-dabiq-isil-161016093547972.html (14.06.2020).

ANNEX

Abstracts

AGNIESZKA PAŁKA-LASEK

Between past achievements and future challenges – Arabic language teaching at the university level

Teaching Arabic as a foreign language faces many methodological challenges connected with the specificity and complexity of the sociolinguistic situation in the Arab world. They mostly concern the necessity for considering different types (registers) of the language, distinguishing, understanding and using which makes it possible for learners to achieve full communication skills.

The end of the 20th and the beginning of the 21st century brought above all a new look at the didactic process, forcing revision of the traditional grammar–translation method in teaching foreign languages. Published in 2001, Common European Framework of Reference for Languages, established by the Language Policy Unit of the Council of Europe, which is a point of reference for the foreign languages curricula developed, became an important spur to changes for the European glottodidactics. It moved the emphasis of education from strictly linguistic competence (systemic knowledge of language) to development of "competence" in a broad sense (including, apart from linguistic competence, general competence as well, which is not connected with language directly, but can be used in linguistic activities).

However, those are not all challenges, which linguistic didactics at the university level has been facing nowadays. Higher education schools must cope with new problems connected with their functioning on the broad market of formal and informal education, which is determined by the term "success on the job market". Needs and expectations of learners change. Which direction will development of Arabic Studies take then? How to bring together the mission of higher education institutions and pragmatic needs of the market, or current needs of "consumers" and guidelines of central curricula. Is such compromise possible?

Keywords: Arabic language, didactics of Arabic, foreign language teaching methods, problems of teaching Arabic language, teaching Arabic in Higher School

IWONA KRÓL

Meanings and functions of genitive constructions in Modern Standard Arabic

I analyse genitive constructions containing substantives (as well as adjectives or numerals following syntactic rules of a substantive) occurring as nomen regens and other substantives as genitival qualifiers – *nomen rectum*. First I discuss phrases with obligatory indefinite substantives as qualifiers because of the meaning of the whole phrase, which I generally define as indicating for an item its "place" in a set of similar items, e.g. آخِرُ يَوْمٍ 'the last day'. The second group of analysed phrases consists of the ones with (obligatory) definite substantives as genitive qualifiers. Constructions of this kind are very frequent in Modern Standard Arabic; semantic relations between their components may first of all be defined as specifying subsets, e.g. مُعْظَمُ البَنَاتِ 'most of girls'. I also discuss phrases in which *nomen regens* performs word-firmative functions, e.g. ذُو وَجْهٍ أَسْمَرَ 'a dark-faced'.

Keywords: Modern Standard Arabic, syntax, genitive constructions, morphological forms, semantics

BARBARA MICHALAK-PIKULSKA

Sultan Qaboos – image of the ruler in panegyrics and elegies of Omani poets

Accession to the throne of His Majesty Sultan Qaboos in 1970 was the real start of a new era in Oman. From the beginning Qaboos underlined that Omani people and their happiness are the most important for him. Qaboos was born on November 18, 1940 in Salalah as the only son of Sultan Sa'īd bin Taymūr and Sultana Mazūn bint Aḥmad al-Ma'shanī. He spend his first years of life in Salalah. When he turned 16, he went to England, where after a period of private education he joined the Royal Military Academy Sandhurst. After passing out from Sandhurst he spend a year with a British infantry battalion on tour duty in Germany. After returning to his homeland, he studied Islam and Omani's history in Salalah for six years.

After taking power, he encouraged the Omanis scattered around the world to return to their homeland and build a democratic state together. During the 50 years of his reign he built a strong, rich, stable and secure state. His visions with passion and conviction were implemented by the Omani people who have free access to health care, education and culture.

Qaboos enjoyed enormous authority all his life. He was always generous and made fair decisions. He put the Omani citizens first, and led Oman to flourish. His reign is considered a golden period in the history of the country.

The 1990s were already a full boom of Oman, both economic and socio-cultural. Citizens live in a beautiful and rich country perfectly managed by Sultan Qaboos. A whole host of poets appear in the literary arena, among which deserve attention: Sa'īd aṣ-Ṣaqlāwī, Sa'īda bint Khāṭir al-Fārisī, Turkiyya al-Būsa'īdī or Ṣāliḥ al-Fahdī. They all share a love for their country and its ruler, what they express in beautiful qasidas.

After the death of Sultan Qaboos on January 10, 2020, a feeling of overwhelming emptiness remained in the nation. The pain remained intensified by every memory of the Sultan and the irreversible tragedy that struck Oman. Omani poets e.g. Sa'īd aṣ-Ṣaqlāwī, Hilāl bin Sayf ash-Shiyādī or Aḥmad bin Hilāl al-'Abri published their elegies. Together they mourned for the passing away of their beloved ruler.

Keywords: Oman, Arabic literature, poetry, panegyric, elegy

YOUSEF SH'HADEH

Microfiction, flash fiction or very short story in modern Arabic literature

In the beginning of the 20th century, Arabic prose developed significantly, after moving away from the traditional writing patterns full of contrived rhymes and unnecessary structural decoration, which appears at the expense of meaning. The new literary genres differed and diversified, and as a result the traits of modern narrative forms became clear. The forms of story varied from long to medium, and from novella to a short story, until a new type was formed which took many terms, the most prominent of which is microfiction, or *qiṣṣa qaṣīra jiddan* (very short story). Since the 1970s, this narrative genre has begun to take a notable place in Arabic prose, which has been recognized by numerous critics and writers. As the Iraqi critic Bāsim Ḥammūdī asserts, the harbingers of the very short story in the Arab world occurred in 1930. This study focuses on examining and analysing various examples from the works of three writers whose stories have expressed the extent of development of this new art, and its constancy as a literary genre clearly defined in modern Arabic prose. The stories studied are samples of works by writers from different Arab countries: Maḥmūd Shuqayr (Palestine), Ibrāhīm Darġūthī (Tunisia), and Muḥammad Ḥijjū (Morocco).

Keywords: Arabic literature, prose, microfiction, flash fiction, flash story, very short story

SEBASTIAN GADOMSKI

In the maze of discourses – monodrama *Bāy bāy Ǧīllū* (*Bye Bye Gillo*) by Ṭaha 'Adnān

Discourse as a term very often appears in contemporary scientific research studies within the humanities and social sciences. We are talking about discourse or discourses in the context of linguistic studies. We refer to the concept of discourse in sociological analyses. The discourse found its place in literary studies, anthropology, political science and many other disciplines. In all of these fields of knowledge, the concept of discourse helps us to describe a number of phenomena and better understand and classify them. However, often in the analyses of linguistic, social, cultural or political issues, we hardly pay attention to a particular, individual man who seems to disappear in the maze of general divagations. This issue is highlighted in Ṭaha 'Adnān's drama entitled *Bāy bāy Ǧīllū* (*Bye Bye Gillo*; 2011), in which the main character – a random individual becomes a victim of social practices, models and mechanisms organizing the world around us.

In my article, by analysing the monodrama of the Moroccan writer Ṭaha 'Adnān, I try to show pluralism and the multitude of discourses that shape our place in the world and affect our life. A wide range of issues related to the problem of discourse and its critical analysis is the background for the presented research.

Keywords: Moroccan drama, Moroccan theatre, Ṭaha ʻAdnān, discourse, critical discourse analysis.

MARCIN GAJEC
Women in Islamic State propaganda

In 2014, the emergence of a so-called worldwide caliphate – Islamic State (الدولة الإسلامية *ad-Dawlah al-Islāmiyah*; IS) under the leadership of Abu Bakr al-Baghdadi was announced. The quasi-state covered significant areas of Iraq and Syria, where Sharia-based laws were implemented. The ISIS creators were very keen to emphasize the pan-Islamic nature of their organization. Their recruiters conducted extensive activities both in the Muslim countries of Asia and Africa, as well as among the Muslim minority in Europe. ISIS propaganda was targeted at a very wide audience and used the most modern means available employing multimedia and the Internet. The main emphasis was on recruiting more fighters who were to participate in the fighting on the Iraqi and Syrian fronts, but some efforts were also directed at attracting the attention of women and girls. Special articles and appeals were to tempt them to join the Islamic State. The role of wives and mothers was foreseen for them, although some of them joined the ranks of the administration, security forces, and even stood up to battle with weapons in hand. This chapter focuses on presenting the efforts of propaganda specialists directed at women. The online magazines *Dabiq* and *Rumiyah* or the Al-Khansa Brigade's online manifesto are excellent examples of such activities and allow to trace significant differences in the message addressed to European women and to the inhabitants of the Middle East.

Keywords: ISIS, propaganda, terrorism, women, Al-Khansa

Managing editor
Zofia Sajdek

Technical editor
Gabriela Niemiec

Proofreader
Helena Piecuch

Typesetter
Marta Jaszczuk

Jagiellonian University Press
Editorial Offices: ul. Michałowskiego 9/2, 31-126 Kraków
Phone: +48 12 663 23 80, Fax +48 12 663 23 83

GPSR Authorized Representative: Easy Access System Europe, Mustamäe tee 50, 10621 Tallinn, Estonia, gpsr.requests@easproject.com

www.ingramcontent.com/pod-product-compliance
Lightning Source LLC
Chambersburg PA
CBHW061803120626
46550CB00005B/2110
* 9 7 8 8 3 2 3 3 4 9 3 3 4 *